Carl Gustav Nieritz, William H Gotwald

The Faithful Missionary

Or, life in Greenland

Carl Gustav Nieritz, William H Gotwald

The Faithful Missionary
Or, life in Greenland

ISBN/EAN: 9783337319045

Printed in Europe, USA, Canada, Australia, Japan

Cover: Foto ©Andreas Hilbeck / pixelio.de

More available books at **www.hansebooks.com**

WINTER IN GREENLAND—"THE SUN ROSE LATE," ETC. (See page 73.)

The Faithful Missionary.] [*Frontispiece.*

THE FAITHFUL MISSIONARY:

OR,

LIFE IN GREENLAND.

From the German of
GUSTAV NIERITZ.

BY

Rev. WM. H. GOTWALD, A.M.

LONDON:
WARD, LOCK, & CO., WARWICK HOUSE,
SALISBURY SQUARE, E.C.
NEW YORK: 10 BOND STREET.

CHAPTER I.
Hans Egede and his Wife 9

CHAPTER II.
The Appointment 26

CHAPTER III.
The Voyage 39

CHAPTER IV.
The Deliverance 55

CHAPTER V.
The Landing 64

CHAPTER VI.
Manna in the Wilderness 73

CONTENTS.

CHAPTER VII.
AMONG THE GREENLANDERS	PAGE 86

CHAPTER VIII.
DANGER AND RESCUE 98

CHAPTER IX.
SORROWFUL EXPERIENCE 118

CHAPTER X.
WHALE FISHING 134

CHAPTER XI.
TREACHERY 149

CHAPTER XII.
COMFORT 164

CHAPTER XIII.
KINDNESS TO ENEMIES 177

CHAPTER XIV.
FEAR AND JOY 187

HANS EGEDE — A SKETCH OF HIS LIFE AND LABORS IN THE DANISH LUTHERAN MISSION AT GOOD HOPE, GREENLAND 201

HANS EGEDE.

CHAPTER I.

HANS EGEDE AND HIS WIFE.

THE young wife of the youthful pastor, Hans Egede, of Vogen, in Norway, came in the greatest haste, with her apron tightly gathered up, from the wood-house into the yard of the parsonage. She hurriedly entered the study of her husband, who, resting his head upon his arm, was thoughtfully reflecting upon what he had just read in a book he was holding in his hand. Mechanically he looked up and noticed his wife, with beaming countenance and sparkling eyes, before him.

"Guess, my dear Hans, what I have wrapped up here in my apron."

Hans Egede must first collect his thoughts before he can be attentive to his wife's request, or notice intelligently what is going on, for he is lost in deep meditation. Observing a black hen that had entered the room close upon his wife's heels, and was attempting to fly at her, he said:

"Even though I did not hear the delicate chirping of the little creatures in your apron, yet this winged betrayer of your secret would tell me that you have young chickens."

"Eight beautiful little chickens," exclaimed his wife, as she, with much apparent satisfaction, opened her apron, — "and all as black as their mother. For some time past I have missed my black hen; I was afraid a fox had carried her off; but as I was picking up chips a few moments ago, I heard a faint piping; I listened, and lo! I found my black hen in the corner of the shed, sitting upon a nest that she had made of straw and sawdust. How fortunate that I discovered the nest when I did! How easily a marten might have devoured the entire little family! See, dear Hans, here are some roosters among the lot that will after a while make delicious dinners for you; and these hens I intend to raise, and increase the number until I have our yard full of fowls. Neighbor Hartman has promised me two pair of pigeons; and we must devise some means by which I will be able to procure some ducks and geese; then we will have a plenty of eggs. So rejoice with me, my good Hans."

"I rejoice with you indeed, dear Gertrude," rejoined Egede, "and especially because I too have discovered a whole nest full — yes, full of black creatures, that, like that brood of yours, have been hid in a corner, and are not yet free from the attacks of hungry enemies."

"Do, then, secure the nest at once," cried Gertrude.

"That I would like, above all things, to do; but to accomplish it I need your consent and assistance."

"Which you have already. Why do you first ask my permission? Where is the nest?"

"In Greenland," responded Egede.

"In Greenland," repeated Gertrude, and in her amazement let the chickens all drop to the floor.

"Yes, in Greenland," replied Egede, courageously. "There, in the most northern regions, live a class of people who have no knowledge of God, nor of his Son Jesus Christ, who are ignorant and superstitious, and are sitting in the regions and shadow of death. These, I yearn to gather under the wings of my pastoral care, as you have gathered the brood in your apron, and to deliver them from the hurtful and destructive snares of

Satan. As upon one occasion there appeared to **Paul** a man from Macedonia, so there appeared to me last night a brown Greenlander, beckoning me, and saying, '**Come** over into Greenland, and help us.'"

"This is nothing **but** imagination," **replied** Gertrude, warmly, "nothing but the miserable result of this constant reading of yours. **To** Greenland, where people's tongues freeze in their **mouths,** and where, instead **of** butter, there **is nothing but** loathsome fish-oil; **no,** say no **more about going** to that dreadful country."

"BONIFACE, many years ago," **replied** Egede, "went to Germany, although the means of subsistence consisted only of acorns, and the entire country at that time was **a** wilderness; and **if** the Greenlanders are enabled to endure the cold in their poor huts, **we** will certainly not freeze."

"Boniface," said Gertrude, **"may do as**

best suits his convenience. He had neither wife nor children, at least not such small ones as ours; and before you seek to help the people of Greenland, aid your poor parishioners here, for these the Lord has entrusted to your spiritual care."

"Very true; but my parishioners here will soon secure another pastor in my stead, and the poor Greenlanders can not. These heathen may much more readily embrace Christianity and serve God than our own people here, who, like the Jews, reject the saving truths of the Gospel, and shun the offers of salvation. Have my sermons and exhortations in any way benefited that old Tittler? Does he not continue to buy and sell the goods taken from poor shipwrecked mariners by the impious inhabitants of the coast?—or is lying less prevalent since I preached my earnest sermon on the Eighth Commandment?"

"Say what you will," said Gertrude, "you will never be able to convince me. When I think of it, that these our dear little ones must go with you to the end of the world, and either be devoured by those horrible polar bears, or frozen to death by the intense cold of that country, I shudder."

"But," replied Egede, a little disheartened, "the Greenlanders also have children, and they endure the cold."

"Yes, and like the young polar bears, they are most likely born with a thick covering of fur," retorted Gertrude.

"You have a misconception of these things, my dear Gertrude. In this book is an account of certain pious persons who, very many years ago, went to Greenland and established congregations, of whom, it is true, nothing has been heard for a long time, owing to the impassable icebergs that have cut off all communication with this part of the country. This author says the cold is not so great and severe as many persons imagine; that grass, shrubbery, and even birch grow there, and—"

"Well, I, your wife, tell you," interrupted Gertrude, with great earnestness, "that I would sooner be separated from you than go with you and the children to Greenland. This, Hans, is my last word on *this* subject. Now you know my decision, and I am determined to stick to it!"

She hastily gathered the little brood together, and, followed by the old hen, left the room. But she soon returned, and through the half open door called to her husband, and said:

"Even this black hen reproves you. She does not leave her nest and her young ones; and *you*, shame on you, Hans—"

Poor Hans, with a heavy heart and with mind all bewildered, gazed with amazement upon the floor, heaving deep sighs. Quite a number of days passed in gloom. Gertrude was sulky and distant, and Egede made no further reference to Greenland. The pastor's wife began to think that her husband had forgotten all about the Greenlanders, although the following play and conversation, which she overheard passing between her two little boys, should have led her to a different conclusion:

"Ugh! ugh!" growled the four year old Niel, as he jumped around the room on hands and feet. "Ugh! u-g-h! I am a polar bear! I'll eat you, Paul!"

"And I," answered Paul, who was one year older, "I am a sea-dog! I swim! Splash! splash! splash! I travel in the ocean; and whenever you want to catch me, I'll dive into the water and away I'll go!"

"Now I'll be a Greenlander," called out Niel, "and I'll throw my javelin on your fur coat. Then you must be covered with blood and swim on your back, and I will fish you up. Then I'll pull off the fur, and make a good feast on your body. Ha! ha! ha!"

"Oh!" cried Paul, "I want to be a Greenlander too! I'll take my boat on my back, and cross the icebergs to the sea, and then I'll sail all around on the water. I'll build myself this very day a little hut like the Greenlanders'."

"Who has told you about polar bears, seadogs, and the Greenlanders?" asked their mother, easily conjecturing who had instructed them.

"Father," they both replied, "he showed us a picture of two Greenlanders, and now we know how they look. They go about clothed in fur skins and with great big caps on their heads. The mother had her little child strapped to her back in a fur hood through which the baby could see just a little."

The mother sighed deeply. "Thank God," she murmured, "you are no Greenlanders, for they have it worse than our dogs, and —" The noise of an approaching conveyance interrupted her remark. Looking through the window, she exclaimed, with joy, rushing out of the house, "My mother, and my cousins!" The children followed her.

A whole cart-load of near relatives drove into the yard of the parsonage. All cried aloud with one voice. It was not, however, a crying for joy, for as they were embracing and greeting one another, the inquiry was made, in a menacing tone, "Where is your husband?" "Where is your husband?" repeated the big cousin, "that stupid Hans?"

Gertrude stared at her cousin thus ridiculing her husband, and rebukingly asked, "**Do you** mean what you said?"

"Indeed I do," he said; "it is to make him a sensible and rational man again that we are here. Where is he?"

In the midst of this large circle of chattering cousins, nieces, aunts, and nephews, Hans Egede, thus inquired after, soon showed himself. Like a flock of hissing geese crowding about a farmer's little boy, so this company surrounded pastor Egede. Above the voices of all the others were heard those of Gertrude's mother and the corpulent cousin.

"My son-in-law," began the mother, "did I give you my daughter that you should have her devoured by hungry polar bears and sharks, or frozen to death? Have you so little love and affection for your children as to sacrifice them to those cannibal Greenlanders?"

"Hans Egede," chimed in the lusty cousin visitor, in a boisterous voice, "we are fully aware of your secret plottings, although you may not know it. Are you so ignorant as to suppose that it will remain a profound secret that you have written to the Bishop of Bergen and Drontheim to commission and send you as a missionary to those Greenland savages? Have you lost your wits, or has Satan possessed and influenced you to leave your congregations and loved ones here, and journey to the end of the world?"

"Yes," added one of the old aunts; "not long ago a whole ship's crew was devoured by those man-eating Greenlanders."

"And the ice, the ice," cried a fourth, "as high as a house! yes, as high as a steeple! swimming everywhere, and grinding ships to atoms, just as the mill-stones do the wheat."

"Frozen limbs," uttered the fifth, "ready for the bears, that are as abundant as sparrows with us."

"The flesh of seals, and fish-oil," said the sixth, "are the only dainties of Greenland."

"And a stove," said an old woman, who seldom ventured out from behind the stove in winter, "is something never heard of there."

Whither should our poor pastor Hans turn; for from all sides came nothing but accusations and reproaches. Even his wife aided the excited relatives in condemning him. Deeply grieved and pained at what he heard and saw, unable to utter a word, he stood motionless, not knowing what course to pursue; and more especially was he almost heart-broken on account of being basely and slanderously charged with desiring to be a missionary only for the sake of the honor and name — when he, from painful experience, knew the deep yearning of his soul was only to do good and preach the gospel of peace and love to the perishing Greenlanders. He vindicated himself by saying:

"Christopher Columbus undertook to discover new countries, and not to spread the kingdom of Christ, and entered upon his arduous task simply for the sake of honor and fame; and who does not commend and bless the discoverer of America? If men hazard their lives in attempting to discover new lands, to unbury the hidden resources of undeveloped regions, why should not I, for the sake of my blessed and divine Master, who has, in his parting words, commanded his ministers to go into all the world and preach the gospel to every creature, baptizing them in the name of the Father, and of the Son, and of the Holy Ghost; why should not I go to Greenland and there gather new witnesses for the truth, and new jewels that shall shine as resplendent stars in the Redeemer's crown?"

At this point a certain ministerial brother now also approached Egede, the minister of their own parish, whom this motley party had induced to come with them, and aid them in persuading our hero to abandon his contemplated endeavor. Taking Egede by the arm, he led him to the window, saying, in a serious tone of voice, "My dear brother in gospel bonds, behold there!" pointing to the huts scattered through the valley, — "to this people you are to preach the Gospel; these are the ones entrusted to your spiritual care, and over these the Lord has placed you as a shepherd to watch and provide. As the Apostle Paul says: 'Let us do good unto all men, especially unto them who are of the household of faith.' As our blessed Saviour was sent only to the House of Israel, so you are sent to these Norwegians, who are greatly in need of spiritual instruction. Christ entrusted the missionary work to his Apostles; so do you permit others, who have no families dependent upon them, and have none but themselves to care for, to go to Greenland."

This last address made a more serious impression upon Egede's mind than all the previous ones. He began to reflect and weigh his project. As those around him now observed that he became a little vacillating, they renewed their persuasions with double zeal. His wife presented the darkest side of the picture in impressive and persuasive language.

Pastor Egede finally acknowledged that he had committed a great mistake, and that he would at once abandon his plans. Nor was this all: he even declared himself freed from a great burden, and that he was indeed sorry to have involved so many of his friends in such great grief on his account. Upon hearing this conclusion, each one present embraced Egede, and rejoiced with him. They all parted in peace.

CHAPTER II.

THE APPOINTMENT.

A FEW weeks after the occurrences narrated in the first chapter, Frau Gertrude sat in her room looking after her husband with tearful eyes, as he was walking out of the yard of the parsonage. Hans had caused her not a little trouble.

The peace of mind which Egede thought he could now enjoy, after being persuaded by his friends that his desire to go to Greenland was the result of his wild fancy, did not long continue.

His attention was again directed to Greenland, and his mind was deeply impressed with the Scripture passage —

"He that loveth father, mother, wife, children, brethren, and sisters, more than me, is not worthy of me."

Conscience is like a fire that cannot be quenched, and like a worm that never dies. With such a fire Egede felt himself being consumed, as well as gnawed by such a worm. His appetite failed him; sleep forsook him; wife and children no longer afforded him joy; and neither in nature, nor in his holy office could he find comfort.

When Jacob's wicked sons heard their father's deep groans, as he lay upon his bed at night, on account of his lost child Joseph, their sleep was thereby disturbed, and they became alarmed under the rebuke of their guilty consciences.

Thus it was with Gertrude. The stings of conscience were keen as she observed the suppressed sighs of her husband, heard the distressing outcries during his dreams, and saw his pale and haggard face after spending so many sleepless nights. Like the brethren of Joseph, who, when they were charged with being spies, and received severe treatment from the ruler of Egypt, she said: "This we have brought upon ourselves, because we are guilty concerning our brother."

Egede also reflected upon himself whenever anything unpleasant occurred. If any person passed unkind remarks concerning either himself or his wife, if a thief stole the grain out of the field, or even if a marten killed a chicken, Egede's invariable remark was, "Why did we not go to Greenland? Why did I not obey the call from God? Why did I do as Jonah, who, on account of his disobedience, was swallowed by a sea-monster?"

Much as these things seemed to disturb Gertrude, she was still more sensibly impressed and alarmed at the distressed countenance of her husband, as he sat by her side at the table trying to eat, but in vain, and, even when with the family, appearing to be unconscious of the presence of his wife and children, and wearing a look that plainly indicated that his heart had been robbed of all happiness. As Egede passed out of the gate, Gertrude arose from her seat, her heart almost breaking with anguish. She went to her husband's study, and searched long and anxiously, until she found a not very attractive-looking little octavo volume, and then hastened back to the family sitting-room.

"This book," she said, with a sigh, "is the cause of all our troubles. Would to God it had never got into my husband's possession. Were it not for it, we would be happy. It must be possessed of some bewitching magic — but only, indeed, for men like my Hans, for me it shall not influence."

She opened it and read the title-page:

"*An Account of Greenland, compiled from*

the Narrative of two Chroniclers, one from Iceland, and the other from Denmark. Published in the Year of our Lord 1674."

She began to read it, and soon was so deeply interested in it that she ceased only when compelled by the evening twilight. Niel and Paul were busily playing "Greenland and Sea-dog," and Hans had not yet returned, although he had started only for an evening walk. Becoming alarmed for her husband's safety, Gertrude went in search of him. A farmer's lad pointed out to her the road to the forest towards which he had noticed the pastor proceed.

Thither she went; and, true enough, she found him upon an elevated plain from which the large timber had all been cut down, the saplings only remaining. Hans was standing upon one of the stumps, and preaching in a suppressed voice to his inanimate hearers. Frau Gertrude listened eagerly, and heard him use the following language :

"My poor, dear hearers, from a far distant country you sent me a message to come and help you. You are my brethren; for, like you, I am descended from our father Adam. Upon you shines the same sun that shines upon my native country, and the same moon dispels the darkness of both lands. But the Sun of Righteousness does not shine upon you. It is cold all around you. Darkness is in your hearts, and has filled them with its chilling influence. Your minds are full of ignorance; you hear no friendly voice saying to you, 'My son, thy sins are forgiven thee.' Nowhere do you hear the joyful message, 'I live, and ye shall live also.' True, when the trumpet of the Judgment shall sound, and earth and heaven be moved, your hard frozen earth shall burst asunder at the fiat of the Son of God. At that day your dead shall arise from their graves, and with bewilderment gaze upon the scenes of that dreadful day; but, alas! they will not know Him who, speaking to His loved ones, shall say, 'Come, ye blessed of my Father, inherit the kingdom prepared for you from the foundation of the world.' They will not hear His voice; but they will be made to feel the power of Him who is ruler of the living and the dead, the saving truths of the Gospel of Jesus Christ. Gladly would I publish to you the blessed doctrine of God's word, but my wife will not go with me. She is a devoted and loving wife, full of sympathy and affection, so much so as to take into her apron a brood of little chickens. Yet you, you who are more, you who are fellow-mortals, my own brethren, to you I dare not point out the Devil's snares. May God forgive her!

"Food is of more importance to her than your welfare, a garment more acceptable than your children, a warm stove more desirable to her than your salvation. Go, wretched Greenlanders, go to your ice-houses, kneel in reverence before your idols, and obey the blind dictates of your sorcerers. My wife wills that I shall not help you. She is a good wife in every other respect, as I have already said, and a devoted mother to my children. I love her fondly, and would not grieve her. But why do you mourn so sadly and weep so bitterly, and make my burden still heavier? Return to your country; there you cannot weep, for your tears would freeze as soon as they would reach your eyes. No whale will swallow me, who, like Jonah, am fleeing from the command of God; but soon the earth will open to receive me, and the grave to conceal me, for I can find no more rest here. I already feel the destroying power of death weighing heavily upon me, and I soon shall be gone. I would that

I could wipe away your tears. Do not weep so loudly." . . . .

A loud, bitter, earnest weeping was now indeed heard, and suddenly two arms entwined themselves lovingly around the pastor's neck, and, with a voice suffocated by sighs and tears, Gertrude falteringly said:

"Oh, my dear Hans, I will follow you whithersoever you go. I will leave not only food, silk dresses, and a warm stove, but more — yes, all. God calls you; let us obey him. Only do not die, but be happy and cheerful again."

From this time Frau Gertrude was not only willing, but exceedingly anxious to go to Greenland. After this hindrance had been now so happily removed, Egede bravely faced and overcame all other serious difficulties in his way. He resigned his pastoral charge, in order personally to superintend, with the king at Copenhagen, the fitting out of ships to Greenland. In preaching his farewell sermon to his congregation, he selected the words of the Apostle Paul (Acts xx. 2), when he preached his valedictory to his congregation at Ephesus. And, as did Paul at the close of the service, so Egede kneeled in prayer with his people, and committed them to the care of their Heavenly Father. There was much weeping and lamentation; many embraced him, many kissed him, and all were sad at the thought of parting; but more particularly sad at his last words, "My face you shall no more see." They all accompanied him to the ship that had previously been sent to carry the missionary to Bergen.

With wife and four children, the youngest of whom was but a year old, Egede landed at Bergen in the summer of 1718, where he was gazed upon as a wonder. Some supposed him full of chimerical notions, others that he was possessed of evil spirits, and had received revelations of the future from them; still others, with whom Egede associated and conversed upon his contemplated mission, esteemed him a man of ripe judgment and of high Christian principles. Three long years elapsed before Egede's designs were accomplished and he was ready to embark.

How remarkable and mysterious are the dealings of Providence with poor mortals, whose life hangs on so brittle a thread! The country pastor, Hans Egede, in the remotest part of Norway, and the restless King Charles XII. of Sweden;—what a singular contrast is presented in the persons of these two individuals! Egede's fond expectations would all have been frustrated, had not an assassin's foul hand deprived the brave Swedish monarch of life in the year 1718.

This occurrence brought back to Denmark the happy quiet it once enjoyed, and encouraged the king to aid the enterprise and equip the vessels necessary for the voyage to Greenland. No satisfactory arrangements would even yet have been effected for the embarkation, had not, through Egede's incessant exertions, a company of merchants been organized to accompany him and open a trade with Greenland. In this way he was able to induce many to go with him, whose only motive was gain and wealth, and not the glory of God or the salvation of souls. To complete this organization, Egede contributed all his own available means, which amounted to some three hundred dollars. The king of Denmark, Frederick IV., pensioned Egede with three hundred dollars annually, and donated him, as a missionary, two hundred dollars for his travelling expenses. The fleet consisted of three vessels. The largest of these was the "Hope," in which Egede and his family sailed, and which was able to accommodate forty-six persons. The other two vessels were a galiot and a whaler. They set sail, but were obliged to return to the haven of Bergen and there anchor until the twelfth of May, 1721, when with a favorable wind they sailed out of the harbor and again ventured on their journey, this time with success. Hans Egede, before his embarkation, was appointed commander-in-chief. In consequence of this, he felt himself under obligations to establish regular religious services, to be observed during their voyage, consisting of a short sermon, singing, and prayer. The difficulties attending an untried voyage, and that too with very small children, the reader may readily imagine.

CHAPTER III.

THE VOYAGE.

HANS EGEDE was sitting in the captain's room with the Holy Bible upon his knee. The family were grouped around him. Frau Gertrude was nursing the babe Caroline, while at her feet lay the little daughter three years old. Paul and Niel, hollow-eyed and weak from a severe attack of sea-sickness, were restless and uneasy, looking thoughtfully now at their father, and now through the little window, through which they could see the ocean's waves breaking upon each other, and hear the howling of the storm.

"Canst thou draw out leviathan with a hook," Egede read; "or his tongue with a cord which thou lettest down? Canst thou put a hook in his nose? or bore his jaw through with a thorn?"

"Father," asked Niel, "what is the leviathan?"

"This no one can tell precisely, my son," replied Egede. "Many suppose it to be the same as our whale; others, that it is the crocodile. But I incline to think that the crocodile is meant, because there are no whales so far south as Job lived."

The door of the cabin was suddenly burst open, true, not by a leviathan, but by an apparently ruthless hand. Immediately a voice was heard.

"Your Reverence, land! land! The long wished-for steeps! land! land! Herr Pastor! Oh, I broke my ribs — I saw it first, your Reverence! Oh, my head! it is the peak of Greenland!"

Whilst uttering these disjointed words, in

rushed a small, broad-shouldered, bow-legged man. With his right hand he rubbed his wounded side and head, and with the left he wiped the tears from his eyes.

"Herr Pastor, oh, that was a fall! I came down from the mast without touching the ladder. But with all my bruises I am the first to sound in your ears, land! land! This deserves *some* reward. All the others are up on deck, ashamed of themselves that I first announced the good news."

Egede closed the Bible reverently, and laid it aside, saying:

"Aaron, it is never prudent to be too rash in doing anything. A wise man will always act cautiously; haste generally brings bruises and wounds, and often more serious results. But come, my dear ones, let us go up and take a view of the land, as the Israelites did the land of Canaan,— as a possession and an inheritance."

With measured steps Egede ascended the stairs, followed closely by his impatient family. At the large mast stood Paul Kitterick, the captain, looking through a telescope into the far off distance. The pastor's family also took a peep, and beheld the wished-for country. It was on the fourth day of June, and just twenty-three days since they first set sail.

The wind, which had been favorable since the twelfth of May, now increased to a storm, so that the strong sails were tried to their utmost; and the ship ploughed deep into the foaming billows. Not far off was the promised land, land that little resembled any country known to the sailors. It seemed low and covered with white and dirty snow, without a single evidence of house or inhabitant.

After another careful observation, Egede addressed the captain thus:

"How our eyes can deceive us; it seems

as though our ship stood still, and as though that coast was approaching toward us."

Kitterick took the telescope and said:

"If you, reverend sir, mean that piece of floating ice, you are right. In less than a quarter of an hour it will have reached us."

"That, floating ice!" repeated Egede; "why, where is the land we saw, Greenland?"

"There," rejoined Kitterick, pointing to the horizon, whose margin was surmounted by what appeared to be dark variegated clouds.

Egede again took the telescope, and examined the distance, and saw that what he had judged to be clouds was truly land.

Joining the sea and the coast were mighty icebergs of wonderful forms, and many miles in extent were girdles of ice, apparently cutting off all communication with the shore.

The ship had now become surrounded by the loose floating ice. The larger pieces seemed almost to baffle the skill of the pilot, while the smaller ones would give the ship an occasional shock which threatened her destruction. Frau Gertrude clung firmly to her husband, while the children were holding to her, until their attention was directed by a sudden noise on the other side of the vessel. Here they first saw, upon a large piece of ice, living animals. Ten of these strange creatures were to be seen upon this floating ice. Some seemed to be sleeping, though they really eyed the ship and the sailors closely, with mouths so wide open that their teeth could be counted.

Aaron the jester was the first to break the silence.

"See here, I rejoice very much, you lords of Greenland and Iceland, to form your acquaintance. How do you enjoy yourselves upon your pleasure trip; how far do you intend to continue your journey?"

"THEY ARE WALRUSES, OR SEA-HORSES," SAID EGEDE.

The Faithful Missionary.] [Page 44.

"These are walruses, or sea-horses," said Egede, addressing himself to his family, " if the accounts I have read of Greenland are correct."

Aaron laughingly called out, " I would love to see those horses gallop! Oh, look at that cunning fellow, who uses his long teeth to walk on, like a lame man with crutches!"

The ice shook beneath the stroke of the walrus as he plunged his huge teeth into it.

In the mean time a sailor had seized a harpoon, and fastening it to the vessel, threw it at a walrus. It penetrated the skin, and stuck firmly in the flesh. The walrus raged and raised a horrible roar, in which the others joined, and made the air ring with their rage. The end of this experiment with these animals was, that all these creatures plunged into the water, and that the sailor with difficulty recovered his harpoon, with a piece of the flesh of the walrus adhering to it.

For a long time an unsuccessful effort was made to find a passage through the belt of ice that girdled the coast. Again and again they tried, but their attempts proved in vain. The fear of encountering a storm, and being frozen fast in the midst of the ice, induced the captain to sail back into the open Atlantic, with the intention of making, at some future time, another attempt to reach Greenland. They thus waited twenty long days. It was with the passengers and crew like with the rich man of whom we read in the Bible: as he saw Lazarus in Abraham's bosom, so they saw the desired land of Greenland from afar; but between them and it was a great impassable gulf fixed.

Kitterick at last lost patience and zeal, and refused to have his vessel any longer as a toy for the freaksome polar sea. "Reverend sir," said he, "the most prudent course for us to adopt is to return home before the summer is ended, and we are frozen between these frightful fields of ice."

"The children of Israel," replied Egede, reproachingly, "were kept in the wilderness forty years, before they were permitted to enter the promised land; and you, after a trial of only twenty days, are full of impatience. You are an old and experienced sailor, at home upon the sea, and yet you would allow a youth, yes, even a woman and innocent children, to influence you to change your plans. What would our people and our most gracious king say should we return home without accomplishing the object of our voyage."

Kitterick submitted to the judgment of the pastor.

As the ship on the 24th of June seemed to be sailing northward, between large bodies of ice, Kitterick inquired of Egede whether, if an opening presented itself, he should run the risk and sail into it. Wind and sea seemed favorable, and Egede, believing that God would deliver them safely from every threatened danger, gave his consent. But they had not advanced far before they discovered the rapidly advancing fields of ice closely uniting, and seemingly forming a solid body of ice, extending the entire distance to the land, which appeared to be about eight miles distant. Driven by necessity, Kitterick endeavored to tack about and extricate the ship from the labyrinth; but his efforts were unsuccessful.

The wind suddenly changed its course, and the storm increased in fury until it raged and drove the ice before it in such a manner as to endanger the safety of the vessel; tossing it, now forward, now backward, now to the right, then to the left, the ship appearing like a plaything that afforded pleasure to the angry storm.

Egede, as did Noah in the ark, sat, during

EGEDE'S SHIPS IN THE ICE, ON THEIR WAY TO GREENLAND.
The Faithful Missionary.] [*Page* 18.

the storm, in the midst of his own trembling loved ones and the other passengers, among whom were several women, concerned not for the ship's cargo, but for his travelling associates. The storm howled without. Upon the ship, the mariners were cursing, the rigging lashed the air, the sails flapped together, and every joint and seam in the ship creaked and groaned. The children cried, the women lamented, and the men lost heart and desired counsel and aid from Egede, as did the Israelites from Moses. They remembered and longed for the flesh-pots of Norway, and mourned with deep grief the day of their departure from their fatherland. Suddenly Kitterick rushed into the state-room.

"Pastor!" he roared out, forgetting in his agitation the usual title of respect, "it is all over with us! Now you can sing the MISE-RERE; the galiot has signalled to us that she has run against an iceberg, and sprung a leak, and is in danger of sinking. Each moment I fear a similar fate for us. You have brought us into this strait; and now, up with you, and give directions how we shall extricate ourselves, if you are indeed a man of God. Why are you spending your time among the women? Hasten to the deck, where we must gall our bones for your sake."

"Thou shalt not tempt the Lord thy God," answered Egede, earnestly; and turning to his murmuring companions, he said:

"The Lord is nigh unto all them that call upon him, to all that call upon him in truth; he will also hear their cry, and will save them."

He then withdrew from the room, and followed the sailor to the deck.

Here sweated and froze, alternately, the sailors at the wheel, at the ropes, and at the sails. Egede cast a mournful look upon the boisterous sea: it was a fearful sight — one beyond description. The ship seemed to be sailing through a narrow channel which had its course in a chasm between rocks thrown together in a chaotic state. These rocks presented a variegated appearance. Here one was dark, there one nearly white, another yellow as a topaz, another of an emerald green; one blue, another somewhat red, and still another dark brown. In the midst of the boiling sea arose a perpendicular wall, higher than the mast of the ship, in the side of which an extended prospect was presented of snow-covered plains, upon which many fierce polar bears were seen stretching open their mouths, and filling the air with their roaring. But this plain was in constant motion, as though the earth under it was in fearful agitation. With a crash and a peal, mountains would disappear, while others rose from the snow-covered plain several hundred feet high! A wonderful scene indeed! The appearance of these rocks was constantly undergoing a change, the crags proving to be nothing but ice. Many of these icebergs near the shore, more properly called ice-mountains, were as deep as the sea itself, and rose above the water higher than the highest church-steeple.

Mythology teaches that at the entrance of the Black Sea there are two movable rocks, either continually approaching each other or receding, thereby imperilling ships which are obliged to sail between them.

Egede saw such rocks now in reality; nearer and nearer they approached each other, with their huge masses threatening instantly to crush their little vessel, their only and last hope. All this Egede saw, and more too, no doubt, in imagination; for he saw the ship crushed to atoms by these icebergs, saw his own body cast into the great deep and torn to pieces by the sea-monsters, and saw the crew becoming a rich feast for the raging bears.

But, lo! in the midst of his revery he espies something which nerves his weakened courage. What is it? A large herd of walruses, that in the midst of the storm were sleeping undisturbedly upon a field of ice. Egede suddenly thought of Christ's expression, " Behold the fowls of the air: for they sow not, neither do they reap, nor gather into barns; yet your heavenly Father feedeth them. Are ye not much better than they?"

Then he reflected further. These irrational creatures know nothing about the mercy of God, and yet they sleep securely under his protection; and you, oh man, whom God created so much nobler than these brutes, and gave you the benefit of his own glorious and precious promises, — which are yea and amen — you are ready to doubt!

Suddenly he turned towards Kitterick, **who** had also seen something, not, however, as the result of pious meditation, but of intoxication.

To his flask of whiskey Kitterick betook himself for refuge when in doubt and uncertainty, and not to a mercy-seat prepared for sinful man.

CHAPTER IV.

THE DELIVERANCE.

EGEDE now left Kitterick and the half intoxicated sailors on the deck, and hastened to the state-room, where the inmates had awaited his return with the greatest anxiety.

"God still lives," he replied to the interrogations of those near him, — "and we also."

He then took the Bible, and read with much seriousness the twenty-seventh chapter of the Acts of the Apostles, closing the reading with these words of the Apostle:

"So God hath given thee all them that sail with thee;" and adding, "I firmly believe that God will also thus deal with us. Had you, my dear friends, faith in our blessed heavenly Father, only as large as a grain of mustard-seed, which, if properly fostered, Christ says, will grow and become so large that the birds can make their nests in the branches, you would feel as safe and secure in the midst of this turbulent sea, as at your homes in Vogen or Bergen."

"I *do* believe," returned Frau Gertrude, with her eyes full of tears, "but Lord, help thou my unbelief."

The Lord *did* send sustaining grace, and that through childish innocence; for Gottfried, who had been closely eying his father, said seriously to his mother:

"Mother, father's wig is on very crooked, the side-curls are on his forehead; and just see, all the hair-powder is out of it! What will the Greenlanders say if they see father in such a fix?"

These words seemed to afford more cheer than a long discourse of comfort. The innocence of the child was communicated to the others. The mother laughed aloud; the father smiled; the other children joined in the laugh, and the grown people in the cabin laughed with the rest. They had almost forgotten, through their fright, to eat or to drink: and now Egede, like Paul, admonished them to satisfy their hunger, and try also to sleep.

The storm still continued; the ship swung back and forth, and seemed tossed up and down by the waves as are balls by sportive school-boys. So the raging elements continued unabated that entire day and the half of the ensuing night.

It was about midnight when Egede awoke from a stupor into which he had fallen, his eyes swollen by weeping. Bewildered he gazed around him, imagining himself in his own dear fatherland — in their quiet and lovely old parsonage. He first observed his true and faithful wife, who, as a hen gathereth her little ones under her wing and sheltereth them, had her arms protectingly extended over her children. The youngest lay in her lap, the others scattered around her; all having their heads touching her. The other passengers were lying about in groups, among whom Egede did not notice the cheerful Aaron. The creaking of the mast, the dimly-burning lamps, and the roaring of the waves, soon restored Egede to full consciousness. He arose to examine into the condition of things. Outside the door of the cabin he stumbled over some one who was sleeping soundly and snoring loudly. It was Kitterick, who had become totally unable to perform his duty through drunkenness. As the pastor attempted to ascend the stairway, a dark object obscured the passage-way, and at the same time called out, "Who comes there?"

The speaker was soon at the side of Egede,

who found himself forced back into the cabin.

"Your Reverence," exclaimed Aaron, rejoicing, "I'll not leave you until you have examined my appearance very carefully. Do you discover nothing new, nothing wonderful in this bow-legged fellow? Don't my shoulders look like wings? Don't my dark complexion appear more than earthly? Do I not resemble Gabriel or some one of the heavenly company?"

"Aaron," responded Egede, gravely, "is this a time to trifle with sacred things, when perhaps the next moment may usher us before the judgment-seat of God?"

"Do not lecture me, your Reverence," replied Aaron, laughingly. "I bring you a happy message; hear me now. When Kitterick had abandoned the ship and given it up for lost, I secretly left this place so that I might not witness the death of your little ones. I passed through the scuttle and fastened my body where I might know nothing of the little world below. I endeavored, too, to prepare myself for heaven, gazing upwards with fixed attention. A huge iceberg intervened and hid the sky, and I was compelled to wait patiently until it had passed by. Beneath me my wooden bed creaked and groaned, and the bending mast made desperate efforts to submerge me in the foaming deep, and force me to make acquaintance with the rising waves. The polar bears and sea-monsters were yelling my lullaby, and the waves were beating time to their song. Frequently I heard Matthews swear, Eric complain, Winlaff pray, and Kitterick whistle. Thus things went on until night closed upon us. The heavenly lanterns were not hung out, and if one did become visible, it was only for a second, for dark clouds soon hid it from view. The fury of the wind ceased, and the waves rocked themselves to sleep. I began then to realize that the ropes had made wounds in my flesh, and the pangs of hunger and thirst reminded me that I was yet a mortal. But come now, your Reverence, and see if I be not a kind of good angel."

Egede ascended quickly to the deck. Here he was able to behold the handiwork of God. The stars shone clear and bright, and the storm that had driven the vessel with such desperate fury among the bergs and fields of ice, had now spent its fury. The exhausted pastor saw a clear and open sea without any icebergs. Full of wonder he stood and admired the view before him. What a change!

"Lord," reverently he broke forth, "thou makest thy angels spirits, thy ministers a flaming fire. Who was it that safely delivered the children of Israel from the host of Pharaoh and changed their lamentations to songs of praise and thanksgiving? Who divided the waters of the Red Sea, and walled them up for a passage for Israel? Thou, O Lord, didst it all. To-day thou dost still testify that thy almighty power is still the same. Each iceberg was more frightful to look upon than all the host of Egypt, and our ship in contrast nothing but a nut-shell, our strongest iron rods but as a straw in comparison to one of these mountains of ice. Who delivered us from the labyrinth of ice and frozen mountains? Who saved us from a watery grave, and from the jaws of the howling beasts around us? Who locked the mouths of the prowling bears from feasting upon our bodies? Our God! our God!! as he did with the lions in Daniel's time, so has he done with them!!!"

Thus Egede soliloquized long before he returned to the state-room to inform the inmates of their safe deliverance.

As the day appeared and the rays of the

rising sun fell upon the shores of Greenland, which was by no means meadow-land, but apparently rocks, snow, and ice, the good ship Hope, and also the galiot, joyfully entered the haven, which they subsequently named Baal's Hunting-ground.

CHAPTER V.

THE LANDING.

BOTH ships had anchored, and the officers and crew had landed, but the passengers remained on the deck of their vessels, and took a view of their new country, which bore no sort of resemblance to their dear native land.

At this moment there came around a neck of land three small boats, containing beings that somewhat resembled men. From a distance they looked rather more like bears with large sticks of wood in their claws. The entire body, from head to foot, was covered with a sack made of seal-skins. Their dusky countenances, visible under enormous fur hoods, presented anything but an inviting

THE LANDING.

appearance. They sat in the middle of their boats, with only the upper part of their bodies exposed, the lower extremities being completely hidden. By means of their double-ended paddles, which they held in the middle, they passed our voyagers with amazing rapidity. Egede, viewing his new parishioners as they were thus near him, almost despaired of ever meeting with success among them.

Aaron, full of sport, said:

"Our future neighbors do not seem to be children of Anak; they are really not any taller than your two sons; we can force such little fellows to embrace Christianity whether they will or not."

The pastor sighed, as he witnessed the miserable condition of these poor Greenlanders, and questioned within himself whether he would be able to enlighten, and bring to a knowledge of the truth, beings so little dissimilar in appearance to mere animals. His answer certainly would have been negative had he not felt that God's spirit would strengthen him and prepare him for this arduous task.

Frau Gertrude also, with her children, was on the deck, and observed the natives. The sight was mutually a novel one, and with astonishment they scrutinized each other's dresses.

After the excitement occasioned by the sudden appearance of the Greenlanders had subsided, an election was held to decide upon a suitable place for a dwelling large enough for all. The location being decided upon, the officers, mechanics, sailors, men, women, and children, went to work with zeal and earnestness. Among this company of fellow-travellers was one merchant, who also acted as clerk to the party — one physician, one smith, one carpenter, one mason, and, we may add, in Aaron, one buffoon. The last named was a singular character. He was witty, had read much, and had studied a whole year, yet had no occupation, having often commenced something and just as often relinquished it. He was vacillating and unstable. At last he was obliged to perform the most menial work in Bergen or starve; therefore to him the expedition to Greenland had peculiar attractions.

Nearly all those composing this expedition were in reduced circumstances, and were induced from selfish motives to undertake this voyage. Morian, the physician, sought for distinction among the Greenlanders, while in his fatherland no one desired his medical aid. Ople, the book-keeper, expected here to become a millionaire. The smith was a drunkard, and had undertaken the journey without counting the cost. Nearly all the others, women and men, were persons of humble circumstances and low station in life.

On the 31st day of August, 1721, the house was ready to be occupied, having been built of stone and earth, and lined on the inside with planks. All the necessary household furniture and provisions were transferred from the ship to their new home. Pastor Egede, as spiritual guide and presiding officer of the colony, deemed it advisable that the installation into their new house should be solemnized with appropriate ceremonies. He appointed a hymn of praise and thanksgiving for their safe arrival to be sung. He had a large circle made in front of the new house, inside of which the entire company was gathered, and he himself appeared among them, clad in his ecclesiastical robes of black, and with his richly folded priestly mantle, inlaid with white, and his snow-white wig.

After singing an appropriate hymn, and offering up a prayer, Pastor Egede preached a sermon from the 117th Psalm, praised God for his great goodness and mercy, asked for a continuation of God's blessings upon them and upon their undertakings, and concluded by reading the rules which were to govern the colony.

A number of the natives, prompted by curiosity, drew near with timidity, to witness these exercises. Although they understood nothing of what was either said or done, yet they noticed that Egede was the leader, from his prominence in all the ceremonies. The most remarkable thing of all, to these dark, fur-clad people, was Egede's white wig, which they gazed upon with amazement.

The new dwelling of our colonists would, in their native land, have been too poor and wretched for even beggars to accept as a home. It was a low, one-story hut, partitioned by rough planks into three apartments, in which the officers, the men, and even the women now resided. A fourth small room was built for Egede and his family alone, and one large stove was made to serve in winter to heat the entire house.

The land upon which the settlement was made, upon close examination, proved to be an island, separated entirely from the mainland, to reach which, boats were necessary.

Egede's first work was to make an examination of the adjacent country, thinking perhaps he might find a more favorable location for a settlement. On the 4th of September, he therefore, with others who were familiar with the use of fire-arms, sailed for Greenland proper. Frau Gertrude with her little children, the other women, and also some of the men, remained. She had much to do and many instructions to give, and was continually anticipating her husband's wants and desires.

The Hope was anchored for the winter in

THE LANDING.

the haven of the same name, the galiot having at once returned to Norway, before the dangerous winter months had begun. Egede on his voyage of discovery soon reached, some three or four miles from where he started, a fine spot of land, with every advantage for improvement and cultivation. In a clear stream of fresh water they found many small salmon, a number of which they caught. The scattered bones of reindeer and seals which they saw lying around, convinced them that the Greenlanders had been there during the early summer. As they ascended the stream, they saw a large herd of reindeer, which, however, catching a glimpse of the sailors, were soon out of sight. But the further progress of the voyagers was suddenly interrupted by the interposition of a huge, rough mountain of ice, that divides the northern part of Greenland from the southern and western.

Upon their return they reached a place where lived five families of Greenlanders, with as many tents made of seal-skins. These people were busy repairing their tents for the approaching winter. As they awaited the approach of Egede and his band, the natives at first prepared to resist the landing of the Danes by a desperate and obstinate resistance, but were disarmed by the boldness of Egede and his men in landing despite their show of opposition. Our good missionary endeavored to conciliate them and others of the natives by subsequently sending them occasional presents. The nearness of the colony was however a dread to the Greenlanders, and they removed further from the settlement. This presented a discouraging prospect for our ardent and zealous missionary.

CHAPTER VI.

MANNA IN THE WILDERNESS.

CONSIDERABLE time had elapsed since the last Greenlander was seen near the settlement. The colonists had rest, and were warned by **the** severity of the winter to confine themselves to their dwelling, and not to venture far away. The north wind roared, the snow fell and drifted fearfully; the masses of ice towered high with a terrible noise around the haven, preventing egress, and walling up the only way to the fatherland.

The sun seemed to sleep too long, for it rose as late as eleven, and after **a** short journey through the heavens, retired at two o'clock. During these short days, in which the very time seemed shorter, idleness framed **for** itself an excuse; every energy of man was dormant, and the earth, the creative earth, was asleep. Therefore, during such a period the seed of evil the more readily took root in the heart and produced a luxuriant harvest of sin.

The book-keeper of the colony was bitterly disappointed. Instead of the great heap of bear, fox, hare, seal, and reindeer skins, — instead of cargoes of fat, train-oil, walrus-teeth, narwhal-horns, and whalebone, which he expected to obtain from the simple Greenlanders for a trifle, — he found nothing but mighty icebergs, which threatened to crush their ship. The surgeon had no person to impose upon, much less to cure. The smith missed the beer-shop; the carpenter's smoking tobacco was all gone, and the mason had by this time consumed his supply of snuff. The sailors were swearing and drinking, instead of praying; the women could not even wash

EGEDE AND HIS COMPANIONS IN WINTER QUARTERS.
The Faithful Missionary.] [*Page* 74.

in the cold, and therefore had no opportunity for gossiping. Had they thought that there would be a scarcity of venison in Greenland, they would have provided themselves with meat and fish before leaving Norway. True, there was a great quantity of wild meat in Greenland, but they knew not how to procure it, for the animals were afraid of man, and did not walk into his arms. On this account, roasts were rare in the new settlement.

One noon, Egede sat with his family around their frugal table in his room. Frau Gertrude placed a dish of water-gruel upon the table, together with a very small piece of meat, the remains of the reindeer last killed. As Egede was asking God's blessing upon their scanty meal, a loud noise was heard in the adjoining room. The cursing was so boisterous, and the pounding upon the table so violent, that the pastor could not hear his own voice.

Rising from the table and opening the door to inquire the cause of the disturbance, he saw the entire company in the greatest excitement. Especially clamorous were the voices of the women. As Egede made his appearance, the smith undertook to speak for all the others and said, in a threatening manner, to Egede:

"Sir, we long since have loathed our food of oats. Where are now the flesh-pots, where the riches of this country, you represented to us? Whom else have we to thank but yourself that we are here walled in as an oyster between his two shells? Of what concern are these benighted Greenlanders either to you or to us? Miserable thanks they will return to you for your efforts to bring them under the influence of the Gospel. No, you will never succeed. You might sooner convert the walruses than this dirty, filthy people. Upon your head we imprecate all the curses possible for our present and future misfortunes."

At the close of this speech a general murmuring was heard, which soon became loud and menacing.

Feeling alarmed for her husband's safety, Frau Gertrude, who with her children had observed through the open door all that was transpiring, rushed out to her husband, the group forming by their own bodies a protection against the imminent danger of violence which threatened the pastor from the hands of the enraged crowd.

Egede motioned imperatively to his dear ones to withdraw and leave him, which they did. Then he stood on a slight elevation, so as to overlook the crowd, and spoke in a firm, manly voice:

"You complain that you have nothing to eat but oat-meal; the children of Israel in the wilderness had manna, quails, and graves.

Be careful, lest by your murmuring you tempt the Lord your God, and the last of these be your portion. You despise these Greenlanders as blind heathen; are you not yourselves such, since you have set your affections wholly on things of the earth? What will be the reward of your earthly labors and anxieties? Earth and ashes; nothing but that which perishes with the using thereof!"

"It is easy for you to preach," replied the rude Plumper, "for you can readily satisfy your hunger, since Greenland furnishes everything you need for yourself; but we poor folks must take and be satisfied with whatever your lordship sees fit to give us. You concern yourself about nothing but how to enrich your own mess, and then even begrudge us our scanty fare."

"Hand me that small piece of meat, if you please, Gertrude." Egede took the plate.

"My good Plumper, I owe you many thanks for reminding me of my duty. Once, as the valiant King Alexander was journeying with his army through a desert, every soldier was parched with thirst and wellnigh exhausted by the march over the burning sand. Alexander dismounted from his horse and walked at the head of his army, willing to share the hardships of his men. One of his attendants having made extraordinary exertions, brought him a little water on his shield, which Alexander took and emptied upon the ground in the presence of the shouting troops, unwilling to drink a drop while there was not enough for all. This heathen king shall not again cause the Christian minister to be ashamed. Here, Plumper, enjoy this bit of meat which my wife had prepared for me. In the future I will have nothing which all do not have."

The smith did not touch the offered dish,

and the others were silent with mortification.

As the weather in the following week was more favorable, Egede concluded to go with the men on a hunting expedition to the place where they had previously found a settlement of Greenlanders. Paul and Niel Egede had so earnestly entreated their father for permission to accompany him that he consented. Arrangements were made to be absent several days, and to quarter in the huts of the Greenlanders until a supply of venison and game had been secured. After a voyage of four hours, they reached the desired landing. They were surprised to find not only the older huts neatly repaired, but a number of new ones built, and inhabited by at least one hundred and fifty persons. Seeing the huts all occupied, gladly would they have returned home, but this they dared not now venture to do, on account of the nearness of the

MANNA IN THE WILDERNESS.

night. They were therefore compelled to ask the Greenlanders for hospitality, which they could only do by signs and gestures.

The Greenlanders, distrustful of the strange intruders, at first did not feel inclined to accede to their wishes; but Egede having shown them by signs that they would certainly perish during the night by the intense cold, they yielded, and allowed them shelter in a distant hut, which had been occupied by two old women whom the natives removed elsewhere.

This winter-house into which Egede and his associates were conducted, was constructed of earth and stone, covered with the slender roots and branches of the oak and willow, upon which was placed frozen turf, making a substantial roof. Neither stove nor chimney was to be seen. Small holes were made through the walls, to answer for windows, which, instead of glass, were covered with very thin entrails of the seal. The door, or curtain rather, was made of a sealskin, which naturally left many openings for the air, to close which the Greenlanders had recourse to many ingenuities.

To their astonishment, Egede and his friends found the air in the hut by no means cold, but filled with a heavy moisture and a horrible smell, which was to the sensitive noses of the Europeans extremely nauseous. A whale-oil lamp, made of stone, was suspended by a string of seal-skins from the ceiling, and hung so low that over the flame the meals of the family were prepared in small kettles of metal, which had been traded for by the walrus-hunters.

"Oh! oh!" exclaimed Paul and Niel, as they entered their new home; and even their heroic father could hardly refrain from utterances of disgust. Aaron held his nose shut and straightway took possession of the only seat in the room; the others were obliged to sit on the ground, if they desired seats at all.

"Whoever is unable to see the usefulness of snuff here," said the mason, as he searched his empty snuff-box for a few grains, "is not deserving of a nose."

"And I," answered the carpenter, "would soon have a different smell in here had I only my pipe full of that good old tobacco. Burnt sole-leather wouldn't smell worse than this horrid stench."

"What is the cause of the loathsome odor?" asked Kitterick.

Niel Egede, who had constituted himself an inspector of affairs, exclaimed, clapping his hands the while:

"It's Aaron's chair! it's Aaron's chair!"

"It's jealousy that makes you say that," retorted Aaron; "you begrudge me my seat because you have none."

The bookkeeper took the lamp and examined the seat which Aaron was so reluctant to leave.

"Yes, this is the cause of it all," he said.

Upon further examination they found that the *settee* upon which Aaron sat so composedly was nothing more nor less than a large lump of walrus-fat that had commenced to melt under the heat of Aaron's body, and which no doubt formed an important part of the larder of the old women who had resided in the hut.

This discovery drove Aaron not only from his coveted seat, but to the far end of the hut, where he began vigorously to scrape his greasy clothes, and rebuke himself for his selfishness.

"Aaron," said Kitterick, "it becomes you the best to remove this Greenland cupboard out of the hut, because you are the only one who had the privilege of enjoying it."

Kitterick's proposition was received with favor by all. Aaron protested, but would have been compelled to do as Kitterick had suggested, had not the Pastor interfered.

"If this be indeed the sustenance of the Greenlanders," said he, "it would be sinful and ungrateful for us to cast the bread of our hosts out of doors. Here, I have found a seal-skin which we will spread over that lump of putrid fat. The manna in the wilderness would also putrefy if it were permitted to lie over night."

"The Lord forbid that we must ever eat such manna as this," whispered the smith to his nearest neighbor. "I would a thousand times sooner live on our hulled oats."

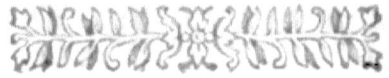

CHAPTER VII.

AMONG THE GREENLANDERS.

AARON summoned courage to take his knife and cut a small hole in one of the windows, to admit a little fresh air, and also to take a view of the country. But the latter was difficult to do, owing to the darkness. He had not long been looking until, in a grievous fright, he exclaimed:

"We have fallen into the hands of murderers; for right in front of our hut three of the Greenlanders are busily digging a deep grave in the snow, without doubt to conceal our bodies after they have killed us."

He again peeps through the little hole in the window.

"Now! ha! they are removing some dead

body to make room for us. See how they work and tire themselves! how they exert themselves to draw it out! Now they have it. What is it? They are filling up the opening."

An irresistible curiosity impelled Aaron to venture out, and even to speak to the suspected murderers.

"Good evening, my good friends! You work diligently early and late. What is that lying before you?"

As he thus spoke, his words of course not being understood, he approached nearer and examined what he had supposed to be a dead body. The Greenlanders did not allow themselves to be disturbed in their labor by his presence. He immediately returned to the hut.

"What was it?" inquired the bookkeeper.

"It was Greenland manna," replied Aaron, with a growl. "A dead seal, full of stench. The snow is their meat-stand."

About an hour afterwards the door of the hut was opened — that is, the skin was pushed aside — and the zealous and kind-hearted natives entered, with their hands full of food, to satisfy to the best of their ability the hunger of their guests. Poorly cooked, strongly-scented seal-flesh, and bladders filled with train-oil — these their dainties — they offered to their visitors.

So as not to mortify or offend their hosts, they all came forward, and Egede first took a piece of flesh from the rude vessel, and raised the flask to his lips, though he did not drink.

They then offered some to Paul Egede, who turned to his father with, "Must I drink out of this? It smells just like the oil with which you used to grease your boots in Vogen. I have enough already from the mere smell."

The Greenlanders seeing with astonishment that the flask was still as full as when they first offered it, and desiring to convince their guests that the train-oil was very good, seized the flask and drank it empty with great relish.

Heaven seemed to punish the colonists for their secret murmurings. Three whole days and as many nights they were compelled by the severity of the weather to remain among the Greenlanders, living upon their loathsome diet, and sleeping upon seal-skins. This disappointment and delay afforded the visitors favorable opportunities of becoming more intimately acquainted with the natives, and also to observe their customs and employments. These heathen, kind and generous, happy and satisfied with their miserable lives, were a constant rebuke to the restless and unsatisfied Europeans, and furnished an example of contentment worthy of imitation by their suspicious and fault-finding guests.

Egede and his sons visited the different huts, and found each partitioned into various apartments by suspended seal-skins, for the separate use of individual families. Some of the occupants had small rooms, others larger ones. Each room had its own train-oil lamp, which answered the threefold purpose of giving light, warmth, and the means of cooking. They experienced very little inconvenience in their huts from the extreme cold, as may well be imagined when we learn that a number of the family, especially the children, sat around the room half naked. The women were busy making various kinds of clothes out of seal-skins and feathers of birds, sewing them together by means of seal tendons and sinews instead of thread. They turned to some use nearly every part of the wild beasts they would kill.

As already stated, seals' entrails were made to supply the place of window-glass.

In one of the huts, where from thirty to forty persons were crowded together, they conducted Egede to a very sick old woman who was suffering intensely with pain, breathing with great difficulty, and scorched with burning fever. Severe coughs, with pain on the chest, seemed to be the only disease of the natives.

With a sympathetic look, Egede thus addressed the sick woman:

"Alas! poor, suffering woman, could you but understand my words, I would offer a cup of consolation that would comfort you in your great distress and sweeten death itself for you. For *you*, the blessed Saviour agonized and died; for *you*, He purchased heaven, conquered death and hell. May that dear Jesus sustain you now in your sickness and pain, and finally bring you to the knowledge of Himself, and to the inheritance of the saints on high."

These words, uttered thus seriously and impressively, engaged the earnest attention of the rest of the Greenlanders, although not understood by them.

By signs they gave Egede to understand that they desired him to breathe upon the woman, that she might recover. Egede would have at once complied with their wish, but he reflected thus:

"I can do no miraculous deed, and would sin did I yield to the superstition of these people and thereby encourage this wicked belief of theirs. God only has power to bless and cure this sick woman."

"Father, do breathe upon her," said Niel. "See how that short fat man tries to show you by his puffed-out cheeks what he wants you to do. The mere blowing can be no sin."

"You do not understand it, my son," said the good pastor, still in doubt.

"Do not hesitate, father," urged Paul. "Blow; you blow the fire to make it burn, and where is the difference?"

Egede then breathed upon the woman, to the great joy of all; saying, as he yielded to their wishes:

"Through my power or might nothing can be done. May our Lord Jesus Christ heal you, and pardon me if by this act I sin. Amen."

During the absence of Egede from his hut, Aaron had formed the acquaintance of one of the Greenlanders in a singular way. Having heard some one mention the name Aaron, this Greenlander, whose name was Aarock, at once joined himself to Aaron, and paid him every attention possible, on account of the similarity of their names. Where Aaron went he went; where he stayed Aarock stayed; what Aaron did he tried to do. This was too much for Aaron. His patience was exhausted; and for the first time in his life he censured his mother for naming him *Aaron*.

Egede determined to take advantage of this little circumstance, and matured a plan for becoming intimately acquainted with these heathen. On the morning of the fourth day, when preparing to leave, Egede took Aaron aside and informed him of his design.

"Aaron," he said, "it seems to me that God by his providence has chosen you to be a missionary to these heathen. You He appoints to prepare the way for usefulness among these people. Answer not as did Moses, 'O my Lord, send, I pray thee, by the hand of him whom thou wilt send.' You have natural qualifications for this work. You shall be my forerunner, preparing the way for me among these benighted people. Consider what a wonderful gift the Apostles received on the Day of Pentecost. They were able to speak with other and foreign tongues, so as to be understood by all of every nation. I, a Moses, stand before the Rock whence the cleansing and healing streams of salvation may flow. The magic wand fails me, and therefore I cannot administer the cordial of life. The Greenlanders are the flinty rock, their language the magic wand, the control of which I have not to unlock their hearts and to move their affections, and have the waters of life flow into them. O Aaron! become like the Aaron among the children of Israel, loosen my stammering tongue."

"Ah! your Reverence," said Aaron, "how can I, since I know nothing of their language."

"Say no more; bridle your tongue, lest you speak something of which you will repent," replied Egede. "I will tell you what to do. You remain here under the protection and friendship of Aarock and learn as many words of their language as possible, and for fear you should forget them, here is my memorandum-book; note in this every word. Try also to find out whether these heathen have any kind of religion, and what they believe. What I thus desire you to do I would most cheerfully myself do, had not the king entrusted to my special care the superintendence of the colony; and I therefore feel unwilling to absent myself so long."

"But suppose, after your departure," said Aaron, "my friend Aarock, from pure love for me, would decide to eat me, what then? No one can tell what may happen here. If I must remain, I'll arm myself with a rifle and a sword."

"'They that take the sword shall perish by the sword,'" answered Egede. "'Confidence begets confidence.' You can retain an axe, not as a weapon of defence, but as an instrument of great usefulness and curiosity to the Greenlanders."

"Your Reverence," begged Aaron, "I sicken at the taste of this train-oil, and my weak stomach revolts at the thought of being fed on stinking fat and oil."

After a number of further objections on the part of the reluctant Aaron, all of which were overcome by the ardent missionary, Egede left with these simple words:

"The Lord be with you, and graciously bless your labors."

Sad and with a heavy heart, though obedient, Aaron gazed wistfully after the departing Pastor.

The homeward-bound colonists found their settlement in great agitation, as will be seen in the next chapter.

CHAPTER VIII.

DANGER AND RESCUE.

THERE are some persons who, when they have once convinced themselves that a certain course of action is right, are firm and unwavering, and perfectly happy in doing what they thus believe to be their duty.

Such a one was Egede's wife, after she saw what was essential to her husband's welfare. Since they had left Vogen, in Norway, not a word of complaint had escaped her lips. With remarkable fortitude and calmness she bore up nobly under the severe trial of leaving her fatherland, trusting to the untried future, and enduring the hardships and fatigues of a long, rough, and dangerous voyage. Not even the prospect of living in a fearfully

"Mother, if you had a crown on your head now, you would look like King David. See, here he is, with a harp and a crown, in my catechism, below the sixth commandment."

"In contrast with King David, your mother is very insignificant," replied Gertrude.

"But he don't sing as sweetly as you, mother," said Sophia, with confidence.

"What makes you speak thus, my dear child?" inquired Gertrude, with a smile.

"I think so because he is a man," replied the child. "The men all *croak* when they sing. Even father, when he sings, says, burr, burrum, burr, burrum, burr, burrum!"

At this expression the women all burst into loud hearty laughter.

"You women need not laugh, for none of you can sing like my mother," replied Sophia, angrily.

"Mother, why don't King David go into the room? It is cold enough to freeze his fingers," said Sophia, after having closely examined her book again.

"It is warm where King David lived," answered her mother. "He cannot go into the room because he is dead."

"Is the Lord Jesus dead, too?" inquired Sophia, examining a picture in which Christ is represented as talking with his disciples.

"No, our Lord Jesus is not dead. He cannot die as you mean, for he is God."

"Does our dear God live yet?" asked Sophia, with wonder.

"Why certainly, or else *we* could no longer live."

"Not long ago I heard father sing —

> 'Oh great and awful need,
> God himself is dead indeed.'"

"By God here is meant Christ," answered her mother. "He was dead once, but now liveth forever."

"Will you, mother, live again when you die?"

"Assuredly."

"And I too, even though a big white bear should eat me up?"

"Yes, my child."

"And Paul and Niel, if they were drowned?"

"Yes, they too."

"And father, if the wild people kill him?"

"Yes; we all shall live again. The Bible says, because Christ liveth we all shall live. How thankful we should be!"

"Will the little rabbit live again, that we ate yesterday for dinner?" continued the child, with a distressed look.

"No, not dumb brutes; only persons like ourselves, who have souls, shall live again," replied Gertrude, to the relief of her daughter.

"Oh, mother, but I am glad. Now I won't be afraid any more of those ugly white bears.

fingers," said Sophia, after having closely examined her book again.

"It is warm where King David lived," answered her mother. "He cannot go into the room because he is dead."

"Is the Lord Jesus dead, too?" inquired Sophia, examining a picture in which Christ is represented as talking with his disciples.

"No, our Lord Jesus is not dead. He cannot die as you mean, for he is God."

"Does our dear God live yet?" asked Sophia, with wonder.

"Why certainly, or else *we* could no longer live."

"Not long ago I heard father sing —

> 'Oh great and awful need,
> God himself is dead indeed.'"

"By God here is meant Christ," answered her mother. "He was dead **once,** but now liveth forever."

"Will you, mother, live again when you die?"

"Assuredly."

"And I too, even though a big white bear should eat me up?"

"Yes, my child."

"And Paul and Niel, if they were drowned?"

"Yes, they too."

"And father, if the wild people kill him?"

"Yes; we all shall live again. The Bible says, because Christ liveth we all shall live. How thankful we should be!"

"Will the little rabbit live again, that we ate yesterday for dinner?" continued the child, with a distressed look.

"No, not dumb brutes; only persons like ourselves, who have souls, shall live again," replied Gertrude, to the relief of her daughter.

"Oh, mother, but I am glad. Now I won't be afraid any more of those ugly white bears.

When we were on the ship, you know, we saw so many on the ice, and I was afraid of their big mouths and long teeth."

"If you are a good and pious girl, you will never need to fear even death itself."

"Why then did father come here to these ugly brown people," asked Sophia, "and not stay with us at our home, if these people will live again?"

"Why, my child, these people are very unfortunate, and your father desires to aid them."

"Tell him, mamma, when he goes to visit them again, that he shall bring me a little brown baby. I will wash and brush it every day until it gets nice and white; and I'll feed it and play with it, and show it all my pictures; and, mamma, I'll tell it all about that black sheep, and—"

Here Frau Gertrude interrupted the conversation by attending to the little one in the cradle.

Although Egede and his associates had already remained absent longer than the appointed time, yet his wife was undisturbed and not in the least alarmed, having unfaltering confidence in the protection of an overruling Providence.

On the morning of the fourth day — the same on which Egede left the settlement of the Greenlanders on his homeward course — the four women of the colonists busied themselves in the preparation of a dinner for their returning husbands.

The men, excepting the bookkeeper, who was engaged in the office, started for the ship to bring thence some necessary things, especially firewood.

"To-day our folks must come home," said Catherine, "or I will conclude they have met with an accident."

As this was said, they heard a fierce growling, and a heavy blow upon the door.

"That is Aaron, the foolish fellow," said Catherine. "I know his silly behavior. He wishes to inform us, before we see him, of his safe return. The smell of the victuals has inclined him to be first in the house and first at the table."

As she thus spoke, she opened the door. With a scream of fright and terror she at once slammed the door shut, but not quite, for a huge white-haired foot, armed with long claws, was thrust in between the door and the jamb, which Catherine, with praiseworthy effort, with all the strength of her body, held closed as tight as possible.

"Help! help! for mercy's sake, help!" she cried out. "A polar bear! he will soon push me back and force his way in."

Two other women pressed with their shoulders against the door; a third, with a piece of wood beat and battered the paw fearfully, without forcing it to give an inch. Gertrude

[*The Faithful Missionary.*]   GERTRUDE THREW THE SCALDING GRUEL IN THE BEAR'S FACE.   [*Page 107.*]

had by this time concealed her infant child behind the large stove.

At that moment, the door, creaking and groaning under the heavy pressure of the dreadful animal, the three women being hurled several feet from the door, an enormous bear entered. Gertrude, with a pot of boiling gruel in her trembling hand, approached the bear, who opened his great mouth, full of large, sharp teeth, showing his blood-red tongue, and expanding his fearful jaws, as though intent on death and destruction.

Gertrude came with faltering step still nearer with the boiling gruel, and gave him a taste of it in his mouth, on his nose, over his jaws, and into his eyes. This experiment was successful. His lordship had from this one experience enough of European cookery. He made his exit in a trice, and the door was instantly closed, locked, and bolted. But the danger was not yet over. The suffering bear, filled with excruciating pains, was still raging in the little entry, and was so savage and furious as to shake the entire house, and threaten to break into splinters the partition-boards, and again enter the room for the purpose of destruction and slaughter.

At last they heard him leave.

And now Frau Gertrude examined things around her. High above the stove perched the merchant, with the loaded gun in his right hand, and holding himself in his uncomfortable position with the left. Catherine, with a firebrand snatched from the stove, stood ready armed for another fight; one of the men had crawled into the bed; little Caroline behind the stove was playing with her toes. All this and more was comprehended by Frau Gertrude in one look.

"Where, where is my Sophie?" she cried.

Not receiving a reply, she hastened with swift steps from one apartment to another.

"O God!" she exclaimed, "where is my Sophie?" as she re-entered the room. Agony of soul was impressed upon every feature of her countenance.

"She went," said a voice from under the bed, "not long ago to bring wood."

"Give me the gun!" exclaimed the distracted mother, springing behind the stove to get the bookkeeper's gun.

But the bookkeeper was unwilling to let her have it, because, should the bear return, he would have nothing with which to defend himself.

"Let me reason with you, woman," he said, from his elevated position above the stove, as he changed the gun from his left hand to his right. "The gun is loaded, and if you jerk it so carelessly you may meet with an accident that may cost you your life. Won't you listen to me, woman?"

"Give me that gun! I will have it!" exclaimed Gertrude, who in her violent struggles forced the coward to leave his place of security to which he had skulked in time of danger.

Frau Egede left the dastard in possession of the gun and advanced towards the locked and barred door to open it and call her daughter, who was in the yard, and help her hasten into the house. She could not see her or hear her voice, and found no trace of her. Defenceless and weak, with nothing to support and nerve her but a mother's warm and never-failing love, prompted and strengthened by a mother's devotion, she determined to rescue her darling child, hazarding her own life. What will a mother not do for her child? But before she had succeeded in opening the door, the other two women attempted to prevent her going out. Her love was too strong for them. Ohle fell down like a dead weight upon the floor, cracking his ribs in the fall, and Catherine was made to measure the length of the planks with her body; but they were soon up again, and at the door, bolting it.

"This woman is stronger and fiercer than a polar bear," said the bookkeeper, as soon as he recovered his breath. "Hark, Catherine! what is that pounding and raging in the other room? It can hardly be that little mischief after whom this woman has rushed with such fury and madness."

Fear blinds, as might be seen from the conduct of Ohle, who had hid Hanke in the trunk, and almost suffocated him, to whose timely relief Catherine now came.

"I can't see at all," continued the bookkeeper, stretching himself up to the window, "what that woman wants out there. Either the bear has already eaten the child or not. If he has, the deed is done; if he has not, maybe he won't find her."

Gertrude scarcely observed the bear, who would roar and sneeze alternately, then scratch his head with his paw and moan pitifully. She flew to the wood-shed near by the dwelling, and searched with eager eyes all around for her dear little one. But she had not need to look long; for she found her lost child quietly seated behind some pieces of wood.

"Keep quiet, child, keep quiet, or the bear will eat us up," spoke the mother as she clasped her Sophia in her arms and pressed a mother's kiss of joy upon her tiny lips.

The bear became more and more restive. He moaned and raged as frightfully as at first. He seemed unwilling to leave the place, and give Gertrude and her daughter an opportunity to return to the house.

The scalded bear was but a cub, and his incessant howling soon drew the mother, accompanied by another cub, to his assistance.

They licked his burns to afford him relief. They then all three commenced anew the attack upon the house.

"Why don't the bear cry so loud any more, mamma?" asked Sophia.

"Be quiet," whispered the mother, "be quiet! Not a word! Should the bears discover us we would be torn to pieces."

"Well, we shall live again," said the child, under her breath, "if they do eat us up."

"But it is so painful to be torn to pieces; and what would father say if he should find us dead?"

"How often must a polar bear bite if he would want to bite my head off?" persisted the little one. "Would he bite more than two times, mamma?"

Gertrude, from this childish talk, imagined she already felt the sharp teeth of these fierce creatures. She pressed the child to her breast anew, and gasped:

"Sophie, pray that God may send his angel to protect us."

"Mother, I am not afraid, since you are with me. The bear won't hurt us. See how often he has run up and down past this wood-pile and never stopped to look at us; and — there, oh, see! The old bear has made a leap, and smashed in a whole window with his claw."

At that moment a report is heard through the opening, and a bullet, shot by the unsteady hand of the bookkeeper, glances over Gertrude's, instead of entering bruin's head.

This shot and the smell of the powder enraged the three brutes still more; and it is wonderful that with their keen eyes they had not yet discovered the place where the trembling mother had concealed herself and her child, who was dearer to her than life.

Gertrude had decided, as soon as she thought the bears should discover her retreat, to upset the wood pile upon herself and daughter, rather than fall a prey to the ravenous and voracious animals. More than once did she lay her hand upon the pile, yet as frequently hesitated to execute her matured plan; when suddenly from two directions voices were heard approaching the scene of conflict, which it now in reality became. Our brave Pastor and those with him, as soon as they came in sight of their uninvited guests, opened a deadly fire. Frau Egede and her daughter were in the greatest danger, being exposed to every shot. Yet true to a mother's love, Gertrude lay herself on her child to shield her, if possible, from a stray shot. One of the young cubs soon fell dead. The other was shot through his heart and lay moaning piteously. The mother bear was unwilling to leave her little ones, but would go from one to the other, licking their wounds and making efforts to help them up;

but all in vain! Yet she chose rather death with her young than to desert them in their death-struggles. The victors soon reached the disputed ground.

Suddenly the smith exclaimed, as he espied Gertrude noiselessly creeping out from under the wood, with her daughter:

"Ha! there's another one that has tried to hide under the wood-pile. Shoot it, quick!"

Gertrude's white apron would have occasioned her death, had not her speech returned quicker than a bullet could reach her. When she was recognized, she was drawn out with great rejoicing, and joyfully embraced by her husband, who was so near losing his noble and devoted wife. After affectionate salutations and greetings had been exchanged, they all turned to view the dead bears. Egede, standing near the dead mother of the cubs, said:

"This wild animal, by her maternal love, has put to shame many a mother. My wife need not, however, be ashamed, for she, by the help of the good God, did more for her child than the dead bear could do for her poor cubs."

CHAPTER IX.

SORROWFUL EXPERIENCE.

"DO you intend leaving us alone again?" inquired Gertrude of her husband, a month after what transpired at the close of the last chapter. "Since our adventure with the bears, I have been more or less afraid when you are not with me," continued Gertrude to her husband, who was making preparations to leave.

"I must go," answered Egede. "You know our blessed Saviour commanded the Apostles 'to go into all the world and preach the gospel to every creature.' So I must go, although I cannot as yet teach these heathen Greenlanders the way of life, for I have not been able thus far to learn their language. Not for the spread of the gospel or the extension of the Redeemer's kingdom did our fellow travellers and associates accompany us to this wild country; but for the purpose of amassing wealth and becoming rich in this world's goods. If we expect to be successful here in winning souls to Christ, and bringing these people under the gospel's influence, we must first place our colony on a firm foundation, and establish a regular trade with our Fatherland; for thus we can obtain means to maintain ourselves and to carry on our operations of Christianizing this people. But I leave you now for still another reason — to bring our Aaron home. I judge he is scarcely able to endure his protracted visit any longer."

"Father, may I accompany you?" asked Paul.

"Not this time, my son. You shall aid me in the work of converting these people, and assist me in bringing them to a knowledge of the truth, by remaining at home, and copying the engravings in our large Bible. The thought occurred to me that perhaps at present I could be more successful in winning these people by pictures and drawings, than by words and gestures.

The Pastor departed with his companions. From three Greenlanders, who had visited the settlers, Egede learned that Aaron was safe and in health. Yet they entreated Egede to come and bring Aaron home.

As Egede reached the settlement of the Greenlanders, where Aaron had remained, the latter came towards the vessel to meet him, in a most pitiable and frightful condition, his face bespattered with blood, and his forehead and eyes bruised black and blue.

He informed them, upon being asked how all this had happened, "that he had bruised and battered himself for the amusement of his hosts, who regarded it as a wonderful feat."

Subsequently, when pressed for the truth of the matter, and Egede had shown him the improbability of his statement, he frankly confessed the untruth, and said, "that for fear of the Greenlanders he made the false report, but that in truth he had been most shamefully abused by the Greenlanders, and that nothing had saved his life but the fear that Egede and his companions would return and punish them for his murder.

"As long as I had anything to give them," continued Aaron, "all went along pleasantly. At last they stole all they could lay their hands on, irritating and tormenting me to such a degree that at last I gave a few of them several slaps on their mouths. That was like pouring fat on the fire. They then cudgelled me until the blood ran off me in a stream, and my only hope of safety was in flight.

And whither was I to flee in this great wilderness? Besides, I had left my axe in another hut, to which I ran, determined to sell my life as dearly as possible. My persecutors, I might almost say murderers, followed me no further than to the door of the hut. Presently an old man came to me, washed the blood from my face and body, and begged me not to inform my countrymen of our fight. Ah, your reverence, you truly gave me a hard nut to crack, when you required me to remain here with these dirty heathen. They are a wicked and suspicious people, whom you will ere long learn to know as such, and upon whom you will realize it is in vain to bestow any labor for their improvement. You need cherish no hopes that they will amend their course of life. If they could do as they desire, they would destroy us root and branch. Mark what I tell you, and then conclude for yourself. One evening, after I had fallen asleep, I was aroused by a screaming, and singing, and shouting, which was being carried on in an adjoining apartment. The rooms were all as dark as midnight darkness could make them, the lamps having all been extinguished. Frightful and alarming was the noise made by one of the magicians, aided by the voices, at one time, of all the men, then of all the women, and finally of all howling together, and calling with savage vehemence upon some unknown power. I trembled and was full of anxious dread. Now, why all this ado? They intend by it to bewitch us out of their miserable country. They have a family god, which, through their superstitions, they believe to be able to do all kinds of work, and which they were frequently consulting as to the nature of our visit to their country, and also whether we did not intend soon to leave it. This favor, your reverence, let us do them. Besides, nothing can be obtained here but wounds and lice, which swarm in every hut. And in summer, if the season deserves that name, you remember well, we are tormented nearly to death by the millions of flies that infest our dwelling!"

"If it be true," began Egede, "what was said and believed by people many years ago, that Satan created flies, hornets, and lice, and every other species of insect that inflict pain upon man to punish the human race, then I might almost conclude that he has gotten a decided advantage in Greenland, and taken entire possession of the country. Of the Almighty God, Creator of heaven and earth, this poor people know nothing, though they seem to be familiar with family gods, magicians, and sorcerers — all of Satan's creation. Something of the law of God is implanted in their breasts, yet they steal, and sin in various ways. Is not this the devil's work? Yet where Satan has his chapel there a church may be built to the honor of God; where Satan has gone about and sown the seed of sin, misery, wretchedness, and eternal death, there also may the seed of holiness, happiness, peace, and life everlasting be scattered. Aaron! Aaron! our ancestors were not behind the Greenlanders in greasy living, in their impiety, their superstition, and their malignity of disposition. Had Ulphilas and Boniface thought of our now happy land in their day as you do now of these Greenlanders, what would have been our condition? Just as Boniface broke down the witchcraft of Germany, so we will endeavor to do here with the household gods and the existing superstition of the Greenlanders — by showing them the inefficiency and weakness of these things, and by publishing to them the power of our God, his love for his people, and his grace and mercy; by telling them of the ability and willingness of Jesus Christ to save us from our sins here, to enable us to live in his fear and his promise after death, and to admit us to the happiness and glory of heaven! But what have you learned of the language of these people?"

"Your reverence," replied Aaron, "it is a most miserable language. Their word for family god is *tongarsuck;* for magician, *augekok;* for God, *Kallok;* for young person, *kojuk;* for reindeer, *lugtu;* for North-star, *kdamersak;* for Pleiades, *killukturset;* a boaster is *mikekau*, etc. It will require a mighty effort to master this barbarous language!"

"Rome was not built in a day, nor does the tree fall by the first cut," replied Egede. "No great deed was ever accomplished without labor and effort."

Instead of giving a reply, Aaron, with a half-malicious smile, pointed to a Greenlander who had just reached the shore with his little boat, and was then approaching their company. His singular appearance excited great wonder, not only among his own countrymen, but among the Europeans. He had on a pair of seal-skin drawers and a garment of the same material over his shoulders, and an outer garment of very singular aspect covering his entire body, of all of which he seemed wonderfully proud. As he came near, they discovered that his flowing dress was made of leaves of printed paper neatly sewed together and bound with fur. It is natural to suppose that this robe, made of such flimsy material, would be full of rents and holes; but none of these seemed to incommode the wearer. With marked attention, as he advanced, the Greenlanders gave place to him. He was an apt illustration of the daw in peacock's feathers, and his experience was no more pleasant than that of the silly bird.

What Aaron, with his keen eye, had from a distance recognized, Egede observed only after near inspection. This garment was the occasion of a very unusual fit of anger to the missionary. He realized how, in holy indignation, Christ, the world's Redeemer, went into the Temple, and after making a scourge of small cords, cast out all them that sold and bought in the Temple, and overthrew the tables of the money-changers, and the seats of them that sold doves. Not through an idle desire to insult the Greenlander did the gentle John Egede rudely tear the paper garment from the heathen, and even make an application of his hand to the fellow's cheek. And wherefore this sudden yet hitherto unmanifested display of anger?

The kindness previously shown by Egede to this Greenlander should have put him to shame. For more than a week had he been at the missionary's house, and enjoyed his hospitality; and when he left, he had stolen Egede's Bible, not to find out the Way of Life, — not to discover his own sinfulness, nor to know that Saviour who died for him, but to make a garment out of it, — a covering for his sinful body. This exhibition of Egede's angry passion can only be apologized for when we remember the age in which he lived, and the attending circumstances calling it forth.

"You blasphemer!" cried Egede. "My Bible! my Bible! The Holy Word of God misused, torn apart, sewed together, worn upon the body, sat upon!"

Egede marched the fellow off. Right over the heart was the twentieth chapter of Exodus, in which the Ten Commandments are recorded.

"Here is written," continued Egede, "'*Thou shalt not steal;*'" and in his heart it was also written by the hand of his Creator.

"Did I deserve such a requital for my kindness to you, you blind heathen? This is Satan's seed! Oh, what a harvest of woe it will produce!"

The poor Greenlander comprehended not one word of Egede's reprimand. The dog cannot understand words, yet he comprehends what we mean. He expresses his joy by wagging his tail, or his shame by carrying it between his legs, after having received words of approval or rebuke. So it was with this heathen thief. Feeling that he did wrong, he received the pastor's blows without attempting to defend himself. He even knelt and tenderly kissed Egede's hand — the hand that had struck him. Egede enjoined upon Aaron to gather the scattered leaves and take them along home.

Not one of the Greenlanders present, attempted to interfere. On the contrary, Egede won their respect by his fearlessness.

The worthy pastor had now overcome his anger, and was sorry that he had struck the poor, ignorant man, and he was not slow to confess it.

He accompanied several of the Greenlanders to where a woman was lying dead. They desired him to restore her to life. He endeavored to show them that no one but God could bring the dead to life again.

As he was preparing to leave the place, his attention was arrested by the crying of a child. He found it near an open grave, wrapped in a seal-skin, and laid there by its father to starve or freeze to death. Its mother was the woman whom they desired Egede to restore to life. Its father had brought it there to die, because he was too poor to support it. This seemed to be a common practice among the Greenlanders.

"Oh, voice of nature! where art thou?" exclaimed Egede, with a heavy sigh. "Even the savage tiger provides for her offspring, and the polar bear would sooner suffer death than desert her young; and man, created in the image of his Maker — man, without a pang, gives over his child to a frightful death!"

Thus speaking, he took the babe in his loving arms.

"You, too, poor little waif," said Egede, "the Saviour bids come to him, that he may give you his grace and salvation. From this moment you shall be my child. Who knows but that perhaps through you your benighted brethren may be brought under the influence of the gospel, and be saved from the wrath to come."

Frau Gertrude welcomed the little one with a mother's love, and Sophia, with great joy, received it under the firm impression that it was her own baby. The bookkeeper and several others murmured, and said that the

Norwegians did **not** contribute their money to establish an orphan's home, but for gain; and that they could now no longer sleep or attend to their duties without being disturbed by the child's crying. Yet Egede adhered to his purpose, and proved himself a true Christian philanthropist.

12

CHAPTER X.

WHALE FISHING.

THE long and severe winter was passed by the colonists in various useful employments.

Egede, who was regarded by the Greenlanders as a sorcerer, made every possible exertion to enlighten and convert them. Whenever Paul Egede's drawings failed, he himself, with chalk, would make certain characters to represent what he desired to teach them. He also, of course, made use of the limited knowledge he had of their language. The doctrine of a future state of existence they comprehended readily, but the doctrine of the atonement they could not understand. Of the immortality of the soul they had quite an intelligent idea. They believed that the good who died would go to heaven, and have as many seal-heads to eat as they wanted. When the northern light becomes visible, they imagine it to be caused by their dead who have come near the earth and are walking about, or else are engaged in playing ball — ball-playing being a common sport among the Greenlanders during their winters. When the moon becomes dark, they say it enters the sea or earth to seize and devour animals and fishes.

"What nonsense," exclaimed Kitterick, on a certain occasion, after hearing this. "We would hardly suppose these people so stupid and ignorant in these things, since they are shrewd enough to steal the reindeer and fishes from before our very eyes."

"Friend Kitterick," replied Egede, "we have still more striking illustrations that man of his own reason and power will not and cannot come to a correct knowledge of God. Did you never read of the Egyptians and their wisdom? Yet they had an ox for their god. Do you know anything of the works of art and skill of the Grecians and Romans, their learning and refinement? *They* believed on gods whom they endowed with attributes that would now disgrace any human being."

Egede directed his efforts especially to correct the common habit among the men and women of lying and deceit. About this time he was successful in effecting two cures among the natives, which advanced him much in their confidence and esteem. One man, who had been afflicted for a long time with sore eyes, and had become blind, he, by means of some simple remedies, was enabled to restore to sight. The other patient he cured of a bad fever. The more Egede grew in popularity among the natives, the more dissatisfied and disaffected and restless did the colonists become.

"Herr Pastor," said Kitterick, "shall we sit here at the fountains of wealth in idle indifference, when the Holland cheesemongers are carrying off the finest whales? Shall we return to our fatherland with empty barrels? Can we satisfy those pecuniarily interested in us with a report of mere words?"

Such and similar complaints were constantly made to Egede by those around him, until he at last consented that a cruise should be made, and that he would accompany the expedition. It was deemed advisable not to venture on the voyage with the *Hope*, but to use a large sloop and several smaller whaling boats. Egede designed by means of this voyage, as they would be necessitated to keep near shore, to form a more general and correct idea of the coast of Greenland, and a more thorough acquaintance with its inhabitants. The worthy pastor was **more** than a mere preacher.

The sloop finally set sail, with all its equipment on board. The boundless icy Polar Sea lay before the sailors. The Spirit of the great God rested upon the mighty waters, and guided the huge icebergs over the deep as easily as the white fleecy clouds in the heavens.

They arrived at a small island, beautiful with its gigantic piles of many-colored ice-blocks piled upon one another. Thus lavishly does God display his almighty power in the grandeur of nature, even where no eye other than his own may see or admire it.

It was early morning, and a heavy fog covered the sea. So thick was it, that the sailors could not see from one end of the sloop to the other, while at their feet roared the foaming billows.

"Yonder are the betrayers of the whales!"

exclaimed Hilliard, one of the sailors, pointing to a flock of birds that now surrounded the sloop and then plunged into the water.

"Those are storm-birds," said Kitterick, "and to us welcome messengers. We will soon hear the whales blow."

The rising sun soon dispelled the heavy mist. The watery horizon bounded a city of ice, through the curved and winding streets of which it behooved the ship to sail cautiously. More than a dozen whaling vessels were scattered through this labyrinth. Many eyes were now on the lookout for whales.

"Stand by to lower!" shouted the captain.

On the instant six men jumped into each of the boats, that were all ready, and took their appointed stations. The man at the bow seized a harpoon, the end of which was fastened to a large strong rope, wound in even coils, and lying in the bottom of the boat; a second managed the rudder.

Soon a tremendous noise was heard, as though a powerful stream of water was forcing its way through a small opening. From the sloop Kitterick observed the huge fish.

"Your Reverence," said Kitterick, "do you observe that fellow in the water there? He sends the water into the air like smoke from a forge. You can see very little of either his head or his back. No 'right' whale blows the water so high as that, nor does it make so loud a noise. Holloa, there! Boat, ahoy! They don't want to hear us. That is a fin-fish. They will be sorry that they did not hear me. Boat, a-h-o-y!"

Is it because the sailors do not want to hear, or is it because the breaking of the waves against the ice makes such a deafening noise that they cannot hear?

The fight now began in earnest. Kitterick had judged correctly. It was what whalemen call a fin-fish — a fiercer and much less desir-

WHALE-FISHING.

The Faithful Missionary.]   [Page 140.

able species of whale. The brown back, and the perpendicular fin upon it, now visible above the water, showed plainly that it was no "right" whale, but really a fin-fish. It was as long as a whale, yet not so thick, and much more dangerous on account of its activity. A second before the oarsmen observed the fish, the harpooner had already sent his iron barb into the fish's head. The mighty creature whirled its huge body half out of the water, like a steed goaded by spurs, and the next instant plunged deep into its natural element. The steersman let go the rudder to take charge of the line at his feet, and see that it was paid out properly. One of the crew had special orders to watch the line as it passed round the "loggerhead." The rope was carried out by the whale so rapidly that it caught fire from friction, and they were obliged to pour on water to extinguish it. Not only did danger present itself from this source, but the boat, from the swift motion of the fish, was in danger of being swamped. Sometimes it was necessary to pay the line out, sometimes to draw it in, just as the fish was near or far off. All on a sudden, the harpooned fish made so deep a plunge that more than one hundred and fifty fathoms of rope were required. The enormous creature drew the boat along with such violence as to cause it to commence filling rapidly with water, and the sailors seeing their lives endangered, found it necessary to cut the rope, and thus lose their booty

This mishap was received with loud cries of disappointment. Kitterick called out from the sloop:

"Just as I expected! These fellows must learn that good rope is worth more than the fish, and—"

At this instant the sloop received a tremendous shock, and the larboard side of the vessel was thrown so high that everything that was not fastened fell pell-mell over everything else, and three of the men — the boastful Kitterick among them — found themselves splashing and swimming in the water, calling aloud for aid. Before Egede's eyes there darted what seemed to be a brown earthen wall alongside the sloop, followed in its course by a stream of blood. Although the men thus plunged into the water could scarcely see, owing to the mixture of blood and water, yet they could distinctly hear the mighty noise. As soon as Egede recovered from the shock, he saw the sailors busy picking up their comrades, and the barrels and other things swimming around. The bleeding leviathan was again to be seen followed by a flock of screaming storm-birds. A second attempt was made to capture him. Another harpoon, from a second boat, was plunged into his body. The suffering and bleeding animal made prodigious efforts to escape from his pursuers. He finally rushed towards a large body of ice near by, hoping to hide his body beneath it.

The men were determined not to be cheated of their booty this time, but held on tightly to the rope, and were drawn with such violence against the mass of ice as to dash their boat to pieces, and hurl them senseless upon it. No sooner had the wounded sailors been brought into the sloop, their heads bound up and their other wounds dressed, than Kitterick addressed Egede thus rudely:

"Your Reverence, you seem to be an unfortunate man. Everything you undertake, both upon land and upon water, is unsuccessful. It seems that you have much to learn. Where the dumb, benighted Greenlanders fill their flimsy boats with all sorts of game, we, with our large vessels, return home empty-handed."

"You may then conclude," replied Egede, "that we are to catch men, and not wild animals and fish. Like Peter, we are to become fishers of men."

"If you could only live then on your people," retorted the bookkeeper. "To preach on other people's money is easy."

"Run the ship up *there* and cast out the nets," said Egede. "I still feel confident that our fishing expedition will be successful."

As the vessel was moving, the bookkeeper began ridiculing this effort too. All at once the attention of those on the sloop was attracted by a singular circumstance.

They observed a long, slowly-moving, gigantic body with a dark back. This monster seemed to have a head the length of the entire body, and a mouth fully as large, with a pair of small eyes situated at the end of the head. This was indeed a "right" whale. No water was spouted through his nostrils; but a deep groaning, accompanied by a roaring noise, heralded his near approach to the anxious and half-terrified sailors.

"Lower away!" shouted all with joy in the midst of their fright, as they gazed eagerly upon the animal, which seemed to be in a dying condition. Upon his enormous back, which emitted a cadaverous smell, sat a flock of storm-birds, eating with eagerness the fat of the poor creature. With sticks and clubs the sailors endeavored to drive off the birds, as they secured the whale to the sloop by heavy and strong cords. Having completed their preparations, they went to work to cut up the whale, piece by piece, so as to get it on the ship.

"This fellow," said Kitterick, "is worth at least one thousand dollars. Do you think we can store it all in our sloop? I fear we will have more trouble than we expected."

Soon, however, this anxiety was removed

from the minds of the colonists, for they now noticed a Holland ship that had approached unobserved.

"Ship, ahoy!" sounded from the deck of the newly arrived ship. "You Norwegian storm-flies! who bid you seize our whale and carry it off? Stop your thieving! It belongs to us by right, and for that matter by might, too."

"Any fool can speak that way," Kitterick replied. "You would like to harvest where you have not sown! Get out with your cheese ship, or we Norwegian storm-birds will pluck out the eyes of you stupid Hollanders."

This uncouth reply called forth a cry of vengeance.

"Bah!" cried a coarse voice, "whose dog are you, that you bark so loudly? Barking dogs never bite. Ho! ho! spread the sails, men, and let us run down that little sloop and drown those thieves."

K

The sailors had not learned courtesy.

It was a fortunate occurrence that their threat was not executed. This Kitterick well knew. Many words passed between both parties, and it was finally feared that the Holland sailors were preparing to run into the sloop. At last orders were given to abandon the whale, and flee for their lives.

The sloop danced on the top of the lofty waves, and was as a toy tossed up and down, threatened with instant destruction. The speed was so great that the vessel began to fill, the men standing in the water up to their waists, busy in dipping it out with every available article, such as hats, boots, etc. Kitterick was very angry as he saw the Holland whalers fish calmly for the dead body they had just been forced to desert.

Egede interrupted his cursing by saying, "The feast was truly prepared, but the guests were not worthy."

CHAPTER XI.

TREACHERY.

THE colonists had anxiously awaited at the opening of the summer the arrival of a vessel from their Fatherland, bringing a supply of provisions, which were greatly needed; but after waiting long and patiently for the relief which did not come, it was decided that the sloop should make a homeward voyage.

Yet not wishing to return home with no gain at all, they concluded to make a cruise to secure seals and walruses, and then return to the settlement. On a clear, warm day, the sun shining brightly, they sailed for a large field of ice, covered with an immense number of seals, that were enjoying their noonday nap in the glowing sunlight.

The sloop was secured to the ice, and the men, with all kinds of weapons, descended as quietly as possible, and began a work of death among the sleeping animals. Aaron came up to Egede, roaring out:

"Who ever christened these sea-calves with the name of *dog?* We might as well call the moon a kitchen-pan. They look about as much like a dog, as a meat-fork does a sausage-kettle. But what do I see? The sea-dogs, as they call them, have fooled us, and are only pretending to sleep. Horrible! What a piggish grunt!"

This time, at least, Aaron spoke the truth.

The seals from far and near prepared, some for flight and others for battle. The assailants raised a murderous shout, which caused the seals to stretch out their necks and to raise their noses as if curious to know what

SEALS ON THE ICE.

The Faithful Missionary.] [*Page* 150.

was necessary to be done. This position afforded the men a fine opportunity to deal deadly blows right and left upon the heads of these animals.

The nose of the seal seems to be almost, like the heel of Achilles, the only vulnerable part. Each blow of the men felled a seal, and very soon the whole field of ice was covered with the dead.

"Why do you stare at me so with your big calf eyes?" exclaimed Aaron, addressing a young seal that was, in its innocence, lying on the ice, unconscious of its nearness to death.

Aaron raised his thick club, and with a blow, aimed at its nose. The blow fell, but not where he had intended; for the weapon struck the cheek of the seal and stuck fast in the fat. Before Aaron had time to secure the club, the seal had, with its sharp teeth, bit it in two, as though it were a stick of candy. With a speed that no one would have supposed the seal capable of manifesting, the enraged animal pursued the frightened Aaron.

"Help! help! or it will tear me to pieces!" he cried, as he ignominiously fled.

Egede ran to his assistance, and only after many thrusts of the spear did the animal yield.

As the sailors were busy flaying the seals and removing the fur and fat, Egede, with Aaron and two others, entered their boat, and, after sailing about for a short time, happened upon some new settlements of Greenlanders, who, having heard of the pastor as a great magician, approached him with marked respect. Accompanied by the Greenlanders, Egede reached a fertile spot, where he observed the ruins of some extensive building.

They answered Egede's "*Kina*" (what is this?) by signs and words, that very many years ago strangers had arrived in Greenland, and in different portions of their country had commenced settlements — built houses, erected churches, and made numerous improvements; but that through pestilence, starvation, and repeated attacks of enemies, their numbers had been reduced more and more, until at last all had died off, and what was here to be seen was all that was left of their homes and churches.

This account was a confirmation of the mournful fact suspected for years in Norway.

History shows that for more than a century Greenland was a part of the Danish kingdom, that it was partly settled by Danes, who had established churches and cloisters. Several bishops were settled there, but the last one sent out was unable, owing to the icebergs, to reach his destination, and was therefore obliged to return home. Since then nothing had been heard of the unfortunate colonists, who fell victims to the severity of the climate and to privation and want.

With quite different feelings and thoughts than those which possessed Marius, when he was sitting upon the ruins of Carthage, was Hans Egede now influenced, as he sat upon the ruins of the dwellings of his ancestors, and even upon the ruins of the houses of God. May not their fate also be ours? thought he. May not the ice form an insurmountable barrier between us and our ship?

But soon these thoughts made way for others. In imagination did this pious man see the only Christian congregation ever established here decrease in numbers day by day, until finally, as at the flood, solitary and alone, only one individual remained to behold the desolation, death had rudely made among his loved companions. He saw this last unfortunate weep bitter tears, heard his groans and lamentations, and felt his agony.

These speechless walls yet standing were silent witnesses of the work of death, of the pestilence as it travelled its circuit, and of hunger and despair as they robbed this last wretched survivor of his life. Perhaps, he thought, this lonely dying one turned a wishful eye to some friend for comfort: then, perhaps, reached forth his weak and trembling hand for some cordial, but no one was near to assist. He sighed and breathed his spirit out. All was now enshrouded in the silence of death. No trace was left of the living; nothing but these massive walls to mark the resting-places of the dead.

One of the company brought Egede a fragment of metal, found in the corner of one of the buildings, and which they judged to be part of a bell.

"Thus is man," sighed Egede, "like the flower of the field; at morning, fresh, rosy, and fragrant; at noon, withered by the sun's scorching rays; and at evening, the wind passing over it, it is gone, and the place thereof knoweth it no more. Blessed truth! we are not to remain here forever. We have a house not made with hands, a city in the skies, whose builder and maker is God. We seek our inheritance above, which is heavenly, eternal; for the sufferings of this present time are not worthy to be compared with the glory which shall be revealed in us. Slumber gently, ye silent sleepers around me! Into your unknown graves will the voice of the Son of God sound, and with Him you shall one day come forth and enter into that kingdom prepared for you from the foundation of the world."

Here Egede was interrupted by Aaron, who said:

"Your reverence, you must come out of this house, for the Greenlanders fear it may fall to the ground and bury you alive. They have also brought several patients here, upon whom they wish you to breathe and lay your hands. This favor you can well afford **to do** for these people. **It costs you** nothing **but a** little breath, **and** how often **do we** waste much of the article in useless conversation. Besides, you can congratulate yourself **that** you are held in such **esteem by the** natives."

Egede complied with Aaron's request, **and** when he saw the sick lying at his feet, whom he was to cure by breathing upon them, and by laying his hands **on** them, he **said, as he** bowed over the first:

"**Oh,** could **I,** like Peter and John, say, 'arise and walk.' May Jesus Christ, the Son of the living God, aid you and grant you restoration to health!"

He then breathed upon him, and laid his hands on him and blessed him; the sick **one** all the time, with a hopeful look and **with a** thankful heart, watching him.

"Do you know," inquired Egede of his companions, "why the blessed Saviour and his Apostles not only taught, but wrought miracles? At that time it was necessary for the ignorant people to see some external proof of what they heard; and these wonderful cures were signs to enable them to believe the doctrines taught them. They desired first to see the working, and then the plan. With us it is different. The kingdom of God must first dwell within us and shine out from within. Then will the truth of the Gospel, after we have an experimental knowledge of it, work wonders for us. The foolish shall be made wise; the spiritually blind and deaf shall be enabled to see and to hear."

"Paul, thou art beside thyself; much learning hath made thee mad," murmured Aaron. "Your reverence," continued he, aloud, "our companions here prefer a piece of meat to your excellent sermon. Besides, it is high time to secure a shelter for the night. It is almost impossible to return to the sloop before dark; and to remain here among these greasy natives is sickening. Let us therefore look for some place of security."

A little later we can see the colonists, some sitting, some lying, under an overturned boat of the Greenlanders. This they found indeed airy, but nevertheless comfortable as a shelter for the night.

The next morning they entered the boat and set sail for the field of ice, where Kitterick had promised to wait for their return. They saw what was left of the many seals they had killed; but the sloop they could see nowhere. Her whereabouts, with the crew on board, remained a mystery to Egede and his party. That day and night was spent in anxious concern, and the next morning the conclusion was reached that a watery grave had received their ill-fated companions.

After having spent the greater part of the following day in a vain search, a consultation was held, and it was decided to return to the Greenlanders with whom they had been the day before, and by offering them a large reward, secure a vessel and a few men to take them back to their settlement, — for without the large boat of the Greenlanders, they thought it impossible to reach their home. The plan was successful. Two Greenlanders, desirous of visiting the settlement, were ready to undertake the voyage.

As they were clearing the little boat, and conveying their things to the larger vessel, they discovered a small store of provisions concealed under a piece of cloth, of which Egede and his companions had no previous knowledge. This circumstance threw a little light, although not a very pleasing one, upon the sudden disappearance of the sloop. Kitterick had deliberately left them to perish, and had, during the night, appropriated this supply of provisions to save them a little longer from starvation. This wicked treachery of Kitterick and his colleagues filled Pastor Egede with pain and sorrow, and his companions with anger and rage.

"Courage, my friends," said Egede to his exasperated associates; "the great and faithful God still lives, and will surely punish such wickedness. Did he not, in this our great need, raise up friends and helpers for us among these heathen? Do you not remember his protection and deliverance granted us in many dangers in which we have formerly been? His good spirit will continue to lead us."

At last they set sail. They had a voyage of at least from fifty to sixty miles to their haven of Good Hope. The natives were encouraged to exert themselves to the utmost to make speed; yet for the want of sails they could not advance rapidly. Six long and tiresome days glided slowly away before they approached Good Hope. First of all, as they neared the haven, they looked anxiously for the good ship *Hope*. She had disappeared from the haven, and was not to be seen. As they realized this, their brave hearts failed them; for they were now left helpless, hopeless, and friendless! Weeping aloud, the three comrades of Egede, and even Aaron, fell to the bottom of the boat, filled with the keenest anguish and the bitterest grief. Egede raised his tearful eyes toward heaven. The sorrow was indeed great to all, and yet it was unequal; for Egede exclaimed:

"Ah! my wife, my children, my all, my all is gone!"

Scarcely could they await the landing, although fearing that their presentiments would be painfully realized. With hasty steps they

EGEDE RETURNS TO GOOD HOPE IN THE GREENLANDER'S BOAT.
The Faithful Missionary.] [*Page* 162.

go in the direction of the house; yet the nearer they approach, the more fearful become their apprehensions. At last they saw from the height down into the valley, where was situated their dear home. It was deserted and still. No sound of the harp reverberated from its walls, no busy scenes were any longer enacted there. All was silent as the grave!

Egede was a mortal as well as his brethren. This could now be seen as he stood there weeping scorching tears of inward anguish. He pressed his hands against his rapidly-beating heart and hastened towards the house, followed by his heart-broken companions.

CHAPTER XII.

COMFORT.

ROUGH, icy Greenland, with its greasy inhabitants and its short summer, and its long dismal winter, had been, nevertheless, a delightful home for Egede, because he had all his loved ones with him. Yet now all of a sudden it appeared to him a dreary country, full of dread and want, frightful to look upon, and entirely under Satan's power. Where now were his confidence and trust in God, and where was that comfort with which he strengthened and encouraged his comrades?

Comfortless, and without knowing what course to pursue, he raised his tearful eyes from the earth and turned them toward his desolate home. See! what is it that now suddenly fills his countenance with an expression of joy, his dimmed eye with new lustre, his tongue with cheerful words, and makes his limbs so strong and his feet so swift?

It is the dove of peace, bringing in its mouth to Egede the olive-leaf. This dove was the homely chimney of the house, and the olive-leaf was the thin wreath of smoke rising above it. How insignificant frequently are the things that either animate us with hope or fill us with despair! This little volume of smoke was to Egede of great moment; for he felt that if any of the colonists survived, these must be some of his loved ones.

With this confident expectation of meeting at least one of his family, he hastened towards the house. But as he stood before the inner door, his courage again threatened to fail him. He listened with a trembling heart. There was a death-like stillness within. Even so it was in Egede's breast; his heart seemed to have ceased to beat. He heard a voice—he listened; he heard a voice of encouragement saying:

"My dear children, pray to our Heavenly Father for grace to bear up under our severe loss, to submit without a murmur."

This voice sounded, at least to Egede, as sweetly as an angel's song, for it was the voice of his own dear Gertrude.

"Peace be with you!"

With this pastoral benediction upon his lips, arising from a heart overflowing with thankfulness to God for what he now beheld, he enters the room and is in the midst of his family. They could not believe their eyes or ears. They supposed it was his spirit; for the treacherous Kitterick had reported that Egede and his companions had been drowned.

And now they that had mourned rejoice, and they that were dead are alive again. O Lord, thy mercy is truly great! They are again and again in each other's embrace. Now what matters the dreariness of the country, the frightfulness of the land, and the scarcity of food? Now all is well. The hut that a few moments before was full of lamentations and sighs, tears and anguish, is now suddenly converted into a temple of praise and thanksgiving.

With great propriety did the others join in this rejoicing; and Gertrude, overlooking the greasy and filthy dress of the Greenlanders, embraced them as angels of deliverance. And these faithful guides had no occasion to regret their visit to the settlement, for Frau Gertrude took special care to see that they received much more for bringing home the lost party than had been promised them.

Besides Egede's wife and children, three

of the women, whose husbands had been on the chase, had remained at home. That no earthly joy has not its bitterness, is clearly seen from the following:

Not only did the treacherous Kitterick carry with him on his homeward voyage nearly all the stock of provisions of the colony, but he also stole three Greenlanders, among whom were two young orphan girls whom Egede had taken to educate and train for future usefulness among their own people.

"For three days," narrated Gertrude, "the sloop came back regularly. As my first inquiry was about you, Kitterick and the bookkeeper informed me that you, with three others, had entered a boat and sailed towards the land, and did not return. With all their exertions and efforts to find you they were unsuccessful, and returned only on account of their own safety. Whether the savages had killed you, or whether you had drowned, what had become of you, they knew not; but because they found your hat, which they gave me, floating around on the water, they concluded you had all perished in the great deep."

"This hat," replied Egede, "is the colored coat which Joseph's brethren found and brought home to their father. The treacherous deceivers! I wore only a cap as I sailed for the land, and then they concealed my hat as a mask for their crime."

"They gave me my choice," continued Gertrude, "either to return home with them or remain here. They said they had enough of Greenland life, and that at home in Norway we were forgotten, for neither men nor provisions were sent us; and that they must make the voyage before the summer was ended. Should I decide to remain, they promised to divide the small stock of provisions with us, and to see that relief should be sent us as soon as they arrived at home. They tore the weeping Navia from my arms, and forced her, along with the other Greenlanders, into the vessel. They acted as though robbed of their reason, and rejected all my counsels, and spurned my protests. They declared that their object in forcing these natives along was for the good of the Greenlanders, and for our good. They said that their presence in Copenhagen would create a sympathy for them, and that they would be educated and brought back as missionaries to their own people. How I spent these three days, since the ship left, you can better imagine than I can tell you. Oh, such misery! Nothing but the sustaining grace of God enabled us to endure the heavy calamity brought upon us. Our Heavenly Father was indeed a present help in our time of need. But now since you are returned to us, and we have you again, my faith has grown as large as a mountain, and cannot be shaken. God will send deliverance!"

"A faithful and loving wife is a great treasure!" ejaculated Egede, as he embraced his Gertrude; "and I have such a treasure! Happiness and peace are the portion of myself and family!"

Egede now took a list of all they had left in the settlement, and counted the number of persons remaining. In all there were twenty-three persons — ten men, four women, and nine children. Only one boat was left them, and provisions for one month.

"Even if Mother Gertrude's confident expectation of receiving provisions during the summer from our fatherland be not realized," said Egede, with a smile, "we need not die from hunger. We must cultivate a fondness for seals and walruses, and, like our brown neighbors, after awhile we will relish them as much as we now do a roasted hare.

We must therefore secure the friendship of the natives, so that, in return for small favors we may show them, they will cheerfully give us a large supply of meat. Thus, when the wild game here has all been shot, there is plenty of food not far off. The many fish that we will also be able to catch will give us a change of diet."

"Your reverence," interrupted one of the men, "we have rifles in plenty, but no powder; for Kitterick and the others took it all along with them. We might as well not have guns. We therefore can't count much on game."

"Yet God has been and yet remains to us an anchor of hope, both sure and steadfast. His Providence is clearly seen in the supply of wood furnished us for our use next winter. In the haven I have discovered a large quantity of drift-wood, which we can easily gather. How wonderful that wood should be found here! In America grows much of the wood with which we warm ourselves; but how much warmth could we have derived from the birch and willow that grow in cold Greenland? Mighty storms uproot whole forests on the mainland of America, and on the tireless back of the great waters these trees are borne to the woodless shores of other countries. In the midst of such wonders should we despond? Far be it from us!"

The following forenoon Paul and Niel Egede sat together in the rear of their dwelling, each one looking the other solemnly in the face.

"My!" exclaimed Niel. "Paul, if you make such an ugly face now, when you only *think* of eating those horrible seals, what will you do when you *must* eat them? Did I make such a face too? I won't want any oatmeal to-day."

"I expect to get to that some of these days, but I can't all at once," answered Paul.

"That meat tastes too bad; even the smell sickens me."

"Oh!" said Niel, "it was just as hard for me. I had to try two or three times before I was able to eat any of it myself. 'All things are possible,' says father, and so I suppose we can learn to eat seals and walruses. The little children of the Greenlanders reach for it with both hands. We can get used to anything."

"I will get over this by and by," replied Paul; "see now whether it will be as nasty some day as it is now; I will be master yet."

Egede drew near, and when he saw his two sons sitting so closely together, he inquired of them what they were doing there.

"We are conquering an enemy," answered Niel, with a laugh.

"You conquering an enemy! how? what?"

"He is invisible — no, not quite invisible after all, for Paul can show him to you," replied Niel.

"Who is he?" again inquired Egede.

"His name is sick-stomach," answered Niel, scrubbing his mouth vigorously.

"What sickens you?" asked their father.

"Because you, father," Paul began, "said that we must use the oatmeal sparingly, and that we must accustom ourselves to seal-flesh, we boiled a piece without your knowing it, and came here to eat it."

"Is it possible?" replied Egede with astonishment, mingled with joy.

"I have gained the victory," exclaimed Niel; "but poor Paul can't keep a straight face when he chews it; he is learning, though."

"Kiss me, my dear children," said Egede. "It may be disagreeable to drink oil, but that is better than starving."

As Egede and the two boys returned into the room, their mother exclaimed:

"My! what makes you smell so badly?"

Their father replied for them, and said:

"This smell is a sweet offering of obedience and submission from our boys, both to God and to us, their parents. Embrace your two sons, even though this smell is offensive. Believe me, dear wife, it is a sweeter odor to me than that of all the spices of Arabia. The children have solved the problem of which you and I were speaking,— how they were to learn to eat seal-flesh and save the oatmeal. Who of us," continued Egede, addressing the other grown persons present, "will be put to shame by the energy and example of children, and not be satisfied with what God's goodness gives us, be it venison, roast hare, or even seals?"

CHAPTER XIII.

KINDNESS TO ENEMIES.

DURING the seven years' famine in Egypt," began Egede the next morning, "the inhabitants bartered their land, their cattle, their all, even themselves, to Joseph for something to eat. They said it is better for us to give up all our property than that we ourselves should die. So must we think, speak, and act. Therefore, my dear friends, gather together everything that we can spare. Such things as glass beads, pins, little knives, needles, etc. With these articles, let us go and trade with the natives for all kinds of provisions, not even refusing seals and walruses. But above all things, be especially careful with our only boat, for it is the sole means by which we can leave our shore. Should we be deprived of it, what then? Go now in the name of God, and fill your hearts with hope. The Lord bless your departure and your return."

The six men left the shore, and ventured on the turbulent waters with their little boat. Egede, with Aaron and the other three men, went to Good Hope to gather drift-wood and take it to their dwelling. As they were busily engaged in this work, Aaron espied in the distance two boats, and in each five men, who were aiming for their haven.

They came nearer and nearer, and finally landed, and gave a mournful account of their having been shipwrecked at a great distance from where they now were, and how many of their shipmates had found a watery grave, and that they alone survived, and were making their way as best they could to the Dutch settlement, at least fifty miles further on.

These ten men were so completely exhausted by fatigue and hunger, that they had scarcely strength enough to walk to the house. With pitiful entreaties, they begged for a little rest and something to eat. With a hearty welcome, Egede invited these distressed and shipwrecked men into his home.

Aaron, with the other three companions, had hastened home in advance of Egede and his guests, and as Egede approached, Aaron called him aside, and said, in an earnest tone of voice:

"Your Reverence, the hour of revenge has come. Do you know who these scoundrels are? These cunning thieves are the very ones who robbed us of our whale, and tried to run down our vessel. Since misfortune has overtaken them they are no longer so boastful. I recognize that fat Bar, and that Horris, and that Schwachter too."

"Well, what do you want to do?"

"Let us invite them into the house, and after our other six comrades return, let us fall upon them some night, and gag them."

"And what then?" inquired Egede.

"Then we can take revenge at our leisure; we can beat them black and blue, and let them nearly die from hunger and thirst."

"Then what?"

"Then, hi! Then we can let them go and meet their fate on the water again; or if we wish, we — can — take — their — lives — by — murdering — them!"

These last words Aaron spoke with a stammer, and with considerable hesitation.

"Then what?" repeated Egede, with a crimson flush in his face.

"Why, then, I think that would be all, of course. What more could be done?"

"Hear me," said Egede, earnestly. "That might be all, so far as these Holland sailors are concerned, but how would it be with *us?*

KINDNESS TO ENEMIES.

Should we do as **you** have just now proposed, **the wrath of** God **would** rest **upon** us, and justly. *He* will punish us for the violation of his commandment, **and** suffer our blood **to be** shed **by** others; will not only visit all this upon **us here, but in** eternity cast us into hell, where there shall **be** weeping and gnashing of teeth. Aaron! Aaron! you want **to** be thought a learned man; you say you have studied the Word of **God, yet** you forget the command of your blessed Master, 'Love **your** enemies; bless them that curse you; and pray for them which despitefully use you and persecute you." Know you not what spirit you are **of? Have not** these Hollanders already been punished for the wicked treatment they afforded us? And you, with their example of God's retributive justice before you, wish to bring a similar punishment **upon** us. Oh, Aaron! I expected better things from you! For **you** to make **God an**

enemy at this time of our great need, would be a double crime. Do you think he has given us this opportunity in vain to do good to our enemies, to manifest Christian kindness towards those who, in their prosperity, despitefully used us?"

Aaron, during this reproof, stood motionless, and neither he nor any of the other three associates uttered a word of complaint as a meal was prepared for the hungry visitors. Even the next morning, after being greatly refreshed by a night's rest, when leaving, Egede gave these ten men a small supply of food for their journey. Aaron never uttered a murmur.

"We have given it not to these Hollanders," said Egede to his companions, "who treated us so brutally, but to the Lord. He will, I am assured, return it to us a thousandfold. Before these, our former enemies, shall have been gone eight days, we will have received

KINDNESS TO ENEMIES.

help. The good Lord does not measure the time for sending us relief by days or hours. Do not you," turning to the Hollanders, Egede continued, "forget our distressed condition after you have safely arrived among your friends. Think of us as being here comfortless and deserted by false friends, and that want will soon press us unless assistance be speedily sent us. Endeavor to obtain relief for us by word and deed. Now depart in peace, and may the God of peace bless you! Be not as Pharaoh's butler, who, after being reinstated in his office, remembered not poor Joseph, but forgot him."

With thankfulness for their kind entertainment, and with many faithful promises to send relief, the Hollanders departed.

Towards the evening of the same day the six men who had gone in search of food returned empty-handed; and after they had learned that Egede had given even of their scanty stock to their former bitter enemies, the departed Hollanders, there arose a general murmuring among the entire colony. They characterized the conduct of Egede as wilful waste, and as taking the bread from the mouths of the children and giving it to the dogs.

The Greenlanders, they reported, met them as open enemies. They refused them permission to land. The proposition to buy provisions was laughed at by the natives; and for their own safety the party felt necessitated to return to the settlement. Egede's position was becoming no enviable one. Scarcely had they provisions enough on hand for one week longer.

In the midst of the company of these murmuring and grumbling settlers, Frau Gertrude made her appearance one morning. Her countenance was beaming, her eyes sparkling with more than earthly lustre, and her voice, as clear and sweet as the ring of silver.

"Why do you sit here and complain, and tempt the Lord your God?" she began. "Shall the confidence and courage of a poor, weak woman surpass that of you strong and hale men. Although no Judith, yet I am the mother of four children, and am not discouraged on account of the untried future. If the Lord had hemmed us in here by gathering the mighty pillars of ice around us, and allowed us neither ingress nor egress, even then we should not repine. Will He not have mercy upon us, even as a father pities his children? Where is your faith, your confidence in God? I tell you, as truly as my Heavenly Father lives, that the oatmeal in the chest shall not be all gone before the help of the Lord is seen."

Egede himself was astonished at the great faith his wife exercised in God, for he himself was finding it difficult to see the **overruling** hand of Providence.

Aaron, in answer to Gertrude, retorted:

"Frau Egede, we in our late journey saw a number of houses in perfect ruins, whose inhabitants had been pious and God-fearing persons, and who nevertheless perished. Are we better than they?"

"Be careful," replied Gertrude, "that your sins be not speedily visited upon you."

"But you are no prophet, for all that," **returned** Aaron.

CHAPTER XIV.

FEAR AND JOY.

FRAU GERTRUDE continued in her happy frame of mind; but the men, on account of their disappointment in not effecting an exchange with the Greenlanders, went about moody and sulky.

Niels and Paul had occasion no longer to sicken over seal-flesh, for the reason that the colonists had none to eat. Egede frequently and longingly gazed over the waters in the hope of seeing some vessel coming from the fatherland to relieve their sore need. It was indeed time, for it was already August, the end of summer and the beginning of the dreaded winter.

One day Egede was amusing himself with

his little foster-child, when Aaron, almost breathless, and in the greatest haste, stumbled into the room.

"Now it is all over with us!" he stuttered.

Egede looked up calmly towards this messenger of bad news.

"More than one hundred large boats, all full of Greenlanders, have just landed at our haven," continued Aaron; "they are armed with bows and arrows, and spears and clubs, and are yelling hideously."

"Let them come," remarked Egede, coolly; "we are in God's hands."

All hastened to the house for security. A consultation was now held, to know what should next be done.

"They are already coming towards the house," cried Hanke, "and are swinging and waving their spears defiantly.

"How is now your courage and faith in God, woman?" inquired Aaron tauntingly of Gertrude. "Do you still believe God will deliver us?"

"Yes," replied Gertrude, emphatically; "for those that are on our side are more than those that are against us. Around our house are armed hosts, and chariots of fire, like those around Elisha at Dathan, to protect and deliver us."

A council of war was now held.

"How many guns have we," inquired Egede.

"Six," answered Aaron, derisively, "with only one load of powder in each. Three swords, two spears, and one child's drum."

"Good," answered Egede, unwilling to notice the jeering tone of Aaron's reply. "But before we go forth to meet the Greenlanders, let us first try to think what may be the cause of this warlike demonstration. To my knowledge we have given no cause for ill-will. I know these natives steal and are under the influence of their sorcerers; but I never knew them to be warlike, or even quarrelsome."

"If this demonstration is really hostile, it is on account of Kitterick and his associates having stolen Navia, Mamor, and Rabba," said Gertrude. "I never expected anything but trouble after those children were stolen."

"Then we must give them to understand," said Egede, "that we are not responsible for that crime."

"I sincerely hope that you will succeed in your plan with these stiff-necked and stubborn fellows," said Aaron, with his usual sneer.

"Hand me my wig and my ministerial robe," asked Egede of his wife. "As a messenger of peace and as a missionary of the Gospel of Jesus Christ, I will first appear among them and endeavor to preach Jesus to them."

Clad in his clerical garb, and with his wig on his head and the Bible in his left hand, Egede, followed by the men, left the house, in which the women and children remained. As they passed into the yard, Egede found himself and his comrades enclosed in a semi-circle of at least fifteen hundred Greenlanders, who were all shouting menacing words and brandishing their weapons defiantly. With measured steps and with fearlessness depicted upon his face, Egede advanced towards the angry Greenlanders.

"Kina?" he called aloud. "What do you want from us? Has any one of us injured you?"

A united response was vociferated:

"Navia, Mamor, Rabba! where are they? Give us the children whom you have stolen from us. Death to you robbers if you do not!"

"The robbers have left," replied Egede.

"They have also robbed us. We are your friends and brethren. I promise you to restore the lost children as soon as a ship returns from our fatherland."

"Navia! Rabba! Mamor!" sounded again from hundreds of voices, so loud that Egede's own words were drowned.

"There, you can see for yourself, the stupid sea-calves!" said Aaron, addressing the pastor. "Are they not like the men of Ephesus, who, for the space of two hours, with one voice cried out, 'Great is Diana of the Ephesians!' If their discordant yelling would only be the end of this ado! But do you see that small crowd of sorcerers over yonder, with fox-legs and bird-claws hung around their bodies, as though determined to supplant you in your priestly office? If only one in this large crowd has the moral courage to shoot the first arrow, all will follow his example, and our fate is sealed. This we must prevent, if possible. If we succeed, we are safe, and they will flee; if not, and die we must, let us die with honor and as Christians."

For a few seconds Egede stood undecided. He could not easily reconcile it to his mind to become a fighting Peter. But he saw that energetic and decided measures must be adopted at once.

"The insignia of my holy office shall not be stained with man's blood. I will doff the priest, and will myself go forward to the fight," said he.

He then laid down his Bible, took off his robe, and, last of all, his white wig from his head; and, lo! the jet-black hair of Egede was exposed to view. With a glance towards heaven for assistance, and a heart full of the keenest anguish, he prayed:

"Father, into thy hands I commit my spirit, and those of my dear wife and children! If I err, lay not my transgression upon my companions."

Then, seizing a sword, he advanced towards the hostile Greenlanders, who, wonderful to relate, are routed, and flee in every direction, as swiftly as the chaff driven by the wind!

With astonishment Egede saw this unexpected sight; but Aaron shouted for joy:

"Your Reverence, it is your WIG that has done it! Your WIG put the enemy to flight! As the brown calves saw you lay aside your white wig, and then saw your beautiful black hair shining out, it was as though an evil spirit had been let loose among them. They regard you as the very chief of sorcerers, and look upon you with fear and dread. But I want to make the rout complete by firing a blank shot after them, and thereby terrify them so much that forever in the future they will leave us in peace."

The shot was made, and, with the report,

Aaron was seen lying on the ground, with shattered knees. The barrel had burst, and Aaron was suffering the reward of his wickedness.

The report of a cannon echoed like distant thunder, from the haven of Good Hope.

Forth from the house ran Frau Gertrude, with quick steps, followed by the other women and the children.

"The Lord has come with His helping hand," cried Gertrude, thankfully.

Unconcerned about the retreating Greenlanders, the settlers all hastened to the harbor. There they saw a cheery sight — three ships weighing anchor, two of stately appearance, and one in a most forlorn and dilapidated condition. The last was the runaway Hope. Overtaken by a storm and tossed about by the waves, she was still fortunate enough to fall in with the other two ships that were on their way to the settlement.

Kitterick informed the officers and the crew, as he had also the women of the settlement, that Egede was dead, and added that the colony had been broken up. Hearing this, the conclusion was formed to return to Norway. But just at this moment a Holland ship came up, with the men on board who had been entertained by Egede, and who reported the truth, and exposed the falsehood and treachery of Kitterick.

Later, as the rich store of provisions was carried to shore, and Egede read the letters sent him, informing him that the King of Denmark would in the future support and maintain the mission; when he saw that Navia, Rabba, and Mamor had safely returned to their native country; when he knew that the Greenlanders felt deep regret at their late hostile demonstrations, and had pledged themselves to good behavior—then Egede's heart was full of gratitude to overflowing. He embraced his wife, who had been so true and so devoted. He lifted his heart to heaven in praise and thanksgiving; and the others who with him were saved from a horrible death, joined in giving to the Lord of lords and to the King of kings the honor due his great and glorious name, in the words:

"Lord God, thee alone we adore,
Lord God, thee alone we thank."

Fourteen long days Aaron was obliged to pay the penalty of his rashness before he could sit at the table with the others, and it was still longer before he was fully restored to health.

Although many difficulties were to be overcome, and many discouragements to be surmounted, yet the colony flourished and grew in strength and importance under the many years of labor, prayer, tears, care and anxiety bestowed upon it by its self-denying and self-sacrificing founder, HANS EGEDE.

The work has continued to progress, until now, after a lapse of a hundred and fifty years, nearly all of Greenland has been won for Christ; and, besides the thousands who have already gone up to see that Saviour whom they here learned to know and love, thousands more are on the way to glory, who will some time shine as resplendent stars in the crown of the world's Redeemer.

Paul Egede walked in the ways of his father — labored in the holy office of the gospel ministry with marked success until the good Master called him to his rest above.

At that great and memorable *last day* that must come to us all, the brown men and women of the far North will arise and call these faithful missionaries blessed, for having taught them the way of salvation.

HANS EGEDE.

A SKETCH OF HIS LIFE AND LABORS IN THE DANISH LUTHERAN MISSION AT GOOD-HOPE, GREENLAND.

CAREFULLY COMPILED FROM VARIOUS RELIABLE SOURCES.

HANS EGEDE, AND THE GREENLAND MISSION AT GOOD-HOPE.

IN pursuance of our plan of first interesting our young readers in *the story*, and then giving them the *history*, we have prepared the following sketch of the life and labors of a devoted Christian man who, one hundred and fifty years ago, left home comforts to preach the gospel of Christ to the poor heathen of ice-bound Greenland. That the sketch may instruct as much as the story has interested you, is the hope and prayer of the writer.

The desirable event of obtaining a firm footing in Greenland, though at last only on the west side, was reserved for the reign of Frederic IV., a prince renowned for wisdom and vivacity in all his undertakings. The person whom God had selected, and certainly called and excited to it in a very particular manner, was Mr. Hans Egede, a clergyman in priest's orders, belonging to the congregation at Vogen in the northern part of Norway.

After this pious man had been a little above a year in the sacred function, in the year 1708, he recollected his having once read, that formerly Christian inhabitants had lived in Greenland, whom the world now no more heard of. Mere curiosity, as he supposed, prompted him to inquire of a friend at Bergen, who had often been on the whale fishery, concerning the present state of Greenland. His answers awakened in him a cordial sympathy for the poor Norwegians, whom he supposed to be still left there, and who, as he feared, were through want of teachers fallen back into heathenism. His philanthropy made him look upon it to be the duty of every Norwegian to search out his forlorn countrymen, and to carry the gospel to them. He thought of various methods how this laudable design might be accomplished. Such musings insensibly gave birth to a desire in his own bosom to be himself instrumental to it. Yet at the first this appeared to be neither allowable nor practicable, because he was already engaged in an office, and had a wife and children and some other relatives to provide for. Therefore he strove to shake it out of his mind; but this made him so uneasy that he knew not what to do with himself, because on the one hand an inward impulse urged him to do it, and on the other hand, not only the trouble and danger of such an undertaking, but a modest fear and scrupulosity of his own presumption intimidated him from it.

At length he thought it would be a proper

medium to make an humble proposal for the conversion of the Greenlanders by some other better-circumstanced persons; grounding his proposition on the Scriptural promises of the conversion of the heathen, on the command of Christ, on the example of the primitive Church, and the pious wishes of many learned men. Still his timidity objected that the proposals to such an important work from such an insignificant hand would be but little regarded, and that it could also scarcely be executed during the war with Sweden, and the great scarcity of money that war occasioned. However, at last he ventured to send away his *memorial* in the year 1710, with a letter of petition to Randulf, Bishop of Bergen, (from which place the trade with Greenland was properly carried on,) and another to Bishop Krog, at Drontheim, to whose diocese he belonged, entreating them to further and support the conversion of the Greenlanders at court in the most efficacious manner. Both the bishops answered him in 1711, commended his Christian intention, promised to do their utmost in his favor, but at the same time represented to him, on the one side the difficulties that attended it, as well as on the other, the advantages that their countrymen, more than any other, might derive from Greenland.

Hitherto the affair had lain, an embryo, in his own breast. But now this epistolary correspondence made it more public than he wished, for it soon came to the ears of his friends, and they set up a vehement opposition against him, and also instigated his wife and family to endeavor to divert him from such a preposterous enterprise, as they were pleased to pronounce this to be. Their remonstrances and tears effected so much, that he really tried to desist from any further thoughts about it, considering that he had done his best, and could not swim against the stream. But that word of our Saviour in the 10th of Matthew, "Whosoever loveth father or mother, etc., more than me, is not worthy of me," brought his mind into such a new agitation and conflict, that he had no rest day or night, nor could any one appease him. In the meantime, by God's overruling hand, a concurrence of troubles so affected his wife that she inclined herself to his counsels. Then he thought: Now is the time to strike while the iron is hot, and he admonished her not to look upon this affair lightly, because in all likelihood God had visited her with afflictions because she could not resolve to renounce everything for His sake. This gave a turn to her mind. She followed his advice, spread the matter before God in prayer, and got an express conviction that she should not run counter to, but follow her husband in his seemingly strange call. Now he believed he had vanquished all his difficulties, and immediately drew up a memorial addressed to the worthy Missions College, and entreated the Bishops of Bergen and Drontheim to promote his request with the utmost earnestness. But they thought proper to advise him to patience till more pacific and favorable times.

In this manner was his project not only postponed from year to year, but also loaded with all kinds of censures.

As to Mr. Egede, these tedious delays tired him out, and he had reason to think that his memorial was not properly enforced; therefore he determined to go himself and prosecute the affair at the proper source. Accordingly he wrote to his bishop that he intended to resign his office, but expected some annual pension from his successor, till he was provided for in Greenland or somewhere else. But as no one would accept of his benefice on these conditions, he relinquished it, notwithstanding, in 1718, with the previous knowledge of his bishop. Yet when it came to taking leave of a congregation he loved, of many good friends, and his near relatives, it gave him some pain; and now his wife, instead of relaxing under the meltings of nature, was obliged to animate her husband, and to strengthen him in his good intentions.

In the interim a report was spread abroad, that a vessel belonging to Bergen had been shipwrecked in the ice on the coast of Greenland, and the crew retreating to the land, were murdered and eaten by the savages. Neither was the frightful tale altogether groundless; yet could it not restrain him, nor the steadfast heroine his wife, from prosecuting their journey with their four small children to Bergen, in order to work their way from thence to a country discredited with such an ill name.

At Bergen he was considered by nearly every one as a monster. Most people gazed upon him as a fanatic. Some few wise and sensible men attended to his proposals of bringing a trade to Greenland into execution. But as the Greenland trade from Bergen had been ruined by the engrossment of so many other nations, nobody was inclined to restore it again, at least as long as the war with Sweden lasted. But just then all of a sudden, through the fall of Charles XII. king of Sweden, in the year 1718, there were hopes of a speedy peace; he embraced the favorable crisis, repaired to Copenhagen, and presented his memorial and proposals to the College of Missions, and not only obtained the joyful answer, that the king would consider of some means of accomplishing this sacred work, but his Majesty also did him the honor of speaking with him himself, and attending to his propositions. Thus he returned cheerful to Bergen, more energetic than ever.

November 17, 1719, a royal order was transmitted to the magistrates of Bergen, that they should collect the thoughts of all the commercial people that had been in Davis's Straits, concerning the Greenland traffic, and should send in their opinions concerning a colony to be settled there, and what privileges the enterprisers desired. But, alas! no one had any inclination for it, and they all described the voyage so dangerous, and the land so disagreeable, that good Mr. Egede and his schemes became almost the mockery of evil tongues. But what could not be effected by the sovereign's aid and mandate to the people at large, that he now endeavored to do by his own private interest, and by speaking with some private merchants.

Thus one year more passed away. At last he was so fortunate as to prevail on a few upright men, who were touched to the heart with his indefatigable zeal, to consent to a conference, and there, by his repeated remonstrances and entreaties, that they would pay a regard to the honor of God, and to their own and their country's advantage, he attained his aim so far, that each of them deposited a capital of about $200, and he himself $300. Immediately he drew up an instrument, which he presented to the bishop and all the clergymen in the city, and also to several merchants, who all made some addition to the sum; and thus at last he got together a capital of about $10,000. After all, this was an inadequate sum; however, a ship was bought called The Hope, to carry him to Greenland, and tarry there the winter. Besides, two ships were freighted, one for the whale fishery, and the other to bring back an account of the new colony. Meanwhile, in the spring, 1721, a joyful account arrived from the College of Missions, that the king most graciously approved of the undertaking, and had favored him with a vocation to be the minister or pastor of the new colony, and missionary to the heathen, with a yearly salary of $300, besides a present of $200 for his equipment.

Thus this unwearied servant of God at last obtained, to his great joy, what he had been laboring after for ten years with great zeal, and amid numberless obstacles, namely, the laborious and perilous office of a missionary among the heathen. In all which he could have no thought of paving the way to a more opulent or honorable post, (for such he had already enjoyed and relinquished,) but was firmly resolved to offer up his life in the cause.

Egede embarked for Greenland, with his wife and four small children, upon the 12th of May, 1721; and he landed in Ball's River, in the 64th degree of North latitude, upon the third of July, in the same year. The company on board the ship consisted of forty persons. They lost no time in building a house of stone and earth upon an island near Kangek, which they called Haabets Oe, or Hope Island, after the name of the ship in which they had made the voyage.

The conduct of Egede as a missionary deserves the highest praise. He conciliated the confidence of the natives, ministered to their wants, learned their language, and gradually introduced some additional rays of intellectual light into their minds.

As soon as he knew the word *kina*, i. e., What is this? he asked the name of everything that presented itself to the senses, and wrote it down. But his children, by continually conversing with the children of the natives, learned the language, particularly the pronunciation, with much more facility than he himself; and he was enabled to make considerable use of their proficiency in the vernacular tongue of the country, in promoting the purposes of his mission.

The trade had a poor appearance in the beginning. The Greenlanders had but little, and the overplus the winter left them they did not choose to barter away with the Danes, because they had been accustomed for many years to dispose of it to the Dutch, who knew the commodities that would go off in Greenland, and could afford them better bargains. In the spring, 1722, a fleet of Dutch ships sailed by the colony, and the Danes saw with vexation how one of them that ran in bought more in half an hour than they could the whole winter.

Even their necessary sustenance began to fail. They had imagined the Greenland fishery and hunting to be better than it was, and provided themselves with but little fish or flesh. And as they were unacquainted with the country, and as the reindeer and hares were shy, and they could scarce catch any fish with their tackle, want began to pinch them before the end of the year, and many were attacked with the scurvy. The people began to murmur against the minister for leading them thither, and as the store-ship stayed away longer in the spring than they expected, they determined to go all away with the ship that wintered there. This reduced Mr. Egede to great perplexity. His conscience would not suffer him to desert a post he had attained after so many years' labor, and which aimed at the conversion of a heathen nation, whereto there was a good prospect. Yet he could not stay alone with his wife and four small children, and see them perish. All that he could obtain from his people was to wait till some time in June for the arrival of the ship, and if it did not come then, and they were resolved to go, they should leave him some of their provisions. But his wife withstood this intention with such courage and constancy, as animated his mind, and put his incredulity to the blush. She would not only pack nothing up, but reprimanded the rest when they began to demolish their habitations, and told them not to make any unnecessary trouble, for she had a positive confidence that a ship was sent out and would safely arrive. The people laughed at the prophetess, but on the twenty-seventh of June they were put to shame, and at the same time rejoiced, by the happy arrival of the ship; and Mr. Egede received encouraging accounts both from the merchants at Bergen, that they would prosecute the traffic notwithstanding its bad aspect, and also from the worthy College of Missions, that it was the king's pleasure to support the mission to the utmost of his power; that he had laid a moderate contribution on all subjects of both his kingdoms of Denmark and Norway, under the name of the Greenland Assessment, which produced a handsome sum.

By these assurances, Mr. Egede was anew incited to spare no trouble or assiduity in anything which might promote the conversion of the heathen, or accelerate the speedy discovery and plantation of the country.

Two deserted children were induced by presents to live with him constantly. Also in the winter a family of six persons begged to take up their abode with him. He saw directly that these people only came to him for a livelihood, neither had he much room for them; and besides, he had already more visits from the Greenlanders than he liked, because they only wanted to see everything, and have some of it given them. However, he took in this family, in hopes of effecting something on their children, and of learning the language. But as soon as the severity of the winter was over, and they had an opportunity of getting something at sea, they removed their quarters; and the two boys that had engaged themselves to live with him constantly, stole away privately one after the other, so that his hopes, and the trouble and expense he had bestowed on them, were all in vain. He had attempted to bring these young people off from a roving to a settled way of life, and to instruct them in the Christian religion, and also in reading and writing; but he soon found that he must be obliged to give them leave to go to sea, or to visit the savages, as often as they had a mind for it. As to their learning, it went briskly at first, because they had a fish-hook or some such thing given them for every letter they learned. But they were soon glutted with this business, and said they knew not what end it answered to sit all day long looking upon a piece of paper, and crying a, b, c, etc.; that he and the factor were worthless people, because they did nothing but look in a book, or scrawl upon paper with a feather: but, on the contrary, the Greenlanders were brave men, they could hunt seals and shoot birds. He took pains to make the advantage of reading and writing comprehensible to them, but this was not so much their concern as temporal advantages; therefore, when they thought they had enough of the latter, they went their way without his knowledge.

In the year 1723, three ships were fitted out for Greenland, one with provision for the colony, by which Mr. Egede received not only the agreeable account which gave hopes of the furtherance of the work, but also Mr. Albert Top as his colleague. The second ship was fitted out for the whale fishery, and returned to Bergen the next year with about one hundred and twenty barrels of blubber from one whale. The value of this and the whalebone amounted to $2,700. The third ship was to have reconnoitred the straits, but neither arrived there nor returned, but was in all probability cast away near Statenhook, where it was separated from the rest in a storm. It was but just before that the crew of a Dutch ship, who had saved themselves in two long-boats, came half starved to the colony.

On this occasion the missionary received an order to send some undaunted sailors to discover the east side of Greenland. Out of concern to see the business faithfully done, he set out himself with two shallops on this dangerous and difficult voyage, although the best summer season was elapsed, in hopes of finding the Straits of Frobisher, and of cutting the way shorter to the east side through the same. The expedition was unsuccessful.

In the beginning of this expedition, the

Greenlanders would not trust the Danes, but put themselves in a posture of defence. But when they understood from the Greenland pilot, that the minister, or, as they called him, the great Angekok (sorcerer) of the Kablunaks, was in the company, they received them with singing and shouts of joy, accompanied them from place to place, and heard with pleasure of the Creator of all things. Nay, their confidence went so far as to conduct the missionary once to a grave, beseeching him to raise the dead, because they had heard so much of the wonderful works of the Son of God, and the future resurrection. They also believed that his invocation and prayer would heal the sick, and once they brought a blind man to him, to whom he should restore sight by touching his eyes.

After admonition to the poor creature that he should believe on the Son of God, he rubbed his eyes with alcohol, and went away. Thirteen years after, the same man came to the colony, and thanked him that he had opened his eyes upon believing his words.

In the year 1724, two ships came from Norway. Besides these two ships, the company, by the king's command, sent another to search out the east side of Greenland, opposite Iceland. But the ice and storms obliged it to return again without effecting anything.

Mr. Egede was busily engaged during all this time, both as pastor and factor. With respect to the mission, having now a colleague, he began this year in good earnest to instruct the Greenlanders. He had translated, as well as he could in this intricate language, some short questions and answers concerning the Creation, the Fall, Redemption, Resurrection of the body, and the Judgment day, and also some prayers and hymns; these he and his colleague read to them, till by hearing several times they could make the answers, and also take in more information concerning them. At first they heard them willingly, but when it recurred too often, they were disinclined, especially if they wanted to go to sea, or had some diversion going on, and were obliged to postpone it till the reading and singing was over. But above all, if an angekok was there, and would practise his incantations, no devotion was then to be thought of; and if the missionaries would still read on, they were only mocked and ridiculed by burlesque mimicry. After much trouble and many expostulations, both of a friendly and a rough nature, they effected so much at last, that they heard their reading with patience, at least did not more treat it with mockery and indolence, nor beat their drum during the singing.

The Greenlanders liked to hear that the soul did not die with the body, that it would receive its body again at the resurrection, without being subject any more to sickness, and that friends and relations would meet again. They were very curious to hear all that he told them of spiritual things, which gave him good hopes. But when a subject had been related to them several times over, and they could not take it in with their gross and carnal minds, they grew tired, and wanted to hear something else that was new, for they imagined they believed already all that he had told them. They were often displeased and petulant when the weather was bad, and attributed it to the reading and praying, because they supposed the air was irritated by this; or they imputed it to their giving credit to the missionary, and not continuing to conform so strictly to the prescriptions of their angekoks, in abstaining from certain meats and employments. Therefore, if they should believe him any more, his prayers must first procure them good weather, an abundance of fish, birds, and seals, and also cure their sick. If he desired them to pray, their answer was, "We do pray, but it signifies nothing." If he told them they should supplicate God chiefly for his spiritual gifts, and for the happiness of life everlasting, they replied, "That we neither understand nor desire; we want nothing but healthy bodies, and seals to eat, and the angekoks can procure these for us." If he told them of the future judgment, and the eternal punishment of hell-fire, they refused to hear anything of it; or they replied that their angekoks knew hell better; or if it even was so hot, yet there was water enough in the sea to quench it, and make it tolerable to them; yea, it would make amends for the cold they had endured upon earth. If he endeavored to convince them of the impositions of the angekoks, that they had never seen any of them go to heaven or hell, because they always chose darkness to veil their legerdemain, then they retorted the question, Whether ever he had seen God, of whom he spoke so much? It was extremely difficult to remove the mistaken conceptions of these people, or to prevent their making a quite sinister use of every truth they heard; for instance, that God was omnipresent, omnipotent, and benign, and that it was his pleasure to help all that call upon him in distress. And as for the corruption of the soul, and its restoration, they could form no idea of it.

Mr. Albert Top had labored four years with diligence and faithfulness in the conversion of the Greenlanders, but his weakly constitution could not stand it out any longer in this inclement country; therefore it was thought proper, before the arrival of the ship, that he should return again to his native country with a Greenland boy, should humbly represent the bad state of the mission, and beg they might soon provide the needful redress.

Mr. Egede gradually found more good-will in the Greenlanders to hear him, and he perceived in those that were dying some seriousness, and also a desire to go to a better place; and those that were healthy increased more and more in faith, as they said, because they had many proofs that God heard their prayer when in danger of their lives, or had nothing to eat. One here and there offered to stay with him; and had he been ambitious of having a parcel of baptized unconverted heathen, he might easily have baptized many; for once as he was instructing them, and had occasion to speak about baptism, they all came and desired him to perform this act on them, and wondered that he scrupled the sincerity of their faith, and of their love to God. But, as he had ground enough for this scrupulosity, because amid all their pretences of firmly and fully believing all that he told them, and their promises of continuing to hear and believe more, he could not observe the least change in their life, nor the least conception or feeling of the corruption of their soul, and consequently no concern, no conviction, and no longing after a happier condition.

He entertained more hope of the children and young people, that he should see Christianity promoted among them in a solid and fruitful manner; and yet it was almost impossible to bring the hopes to accomplishment, because he could not give these youthful minds due instruction and attendance, on account of the continual peregrinations of their parents.

Meanwhile, Mr. Egede held a conference with his two colleagues, in which he laid before them a written proposal, that, as he saw, for want of proper regulations, nothing was to be effected among the adult Greenlanders, but to gain their cold assent to the Word, without any reflection on their misery or any desire after grace; and yet he did not like to spend his time without fruit, and could much less bear to see poor innocent children die without baptism: therefore he had come to a conclusion in the presence of God, to make such children partakers of holy baptism, whose parents gave their assent to the true religion, in hopes that the parents would stay in the neighborhood, and let their children be taught hereafter the knowledge and fear of God by capable instructors.

Accordingly, Mr. Egede made the beginning in Kokœrnen, February 11th, 1729, with sixteen children, whose parents not only consented to it, but also begged to be baptized themselves. He proceeded to baptize the children on the rest of the islands, as also in his former dwelling-place at Kangek, and says, that there were some among them who could answer intelligently to the questions asked them.

By the ships tarrying very late in 1730 before their arrival, they fell once more into great embarrassment about provisions, which was heightened by the loss of a shallop near Good Hope, loaded with provisions, with which one man was lost. A boat that went to his assistance was also wrecked among the ice, and the rest of the provisions in another shallop were obliged to be thrown mostly into the sea to save the people. However, at last, on the 2d of September, the ship arrived safe at Good Hope, but because the winter was at the door, it could not go to Nepisene. All sorts of building-materials were sent by this ship to erect houses in the valleys where the Norwegians formerly lived, and they were to be inhabited by families from Iceland.

But, alas! all these projects, carried on with so much ardor, labor, and expense, seemed all at once to receive their mortal blow by the death of King Frederic IV. in this year. For when the government under Christian VI. saw no way how the sums expended for so many years, and still wanted, could be reimbursed by the trade and erection of the colonies, and besides, that the conversion of the infidels had yielded such an unfavorable prospect for these ten years past; for these reasons a royal mandate was transmitted by the ship in 1731, that both the colonies should be relinquished, and all the people should return.

In such a state of the case, no one could resolve to stay with Mr. Egede. On account of these and other heavy circumstances, which threatened the ruin of the mission, he was obliged to suspend entirely the baptism of the Greenland children, not only because he was uncertain how long he himself might stay to take care of their Christian education, but chiefly because he saw that nothing was to be done with the parents.

Besides, such a series of labor, vexation, and anxiety, had so harassed and worn out the missionary, and a disorder on his breast lay so heavy upon him, that he could not well travel about among the heathen as he had done, but was compelled to resign the instruction of them mostly to his son, and he to do it only occasionally when he went about trading for the products of the country.

Mr. Egede, having thus been in suspense between hope and fear for two years, was at last rejoiced at the ship's arrival, May 20, 1733, with the intimation that the Greenland trade should be begun anew, and the mission supported; for which service the king was graciously pleased to order a free gift of $2000 annually.

With this ship arrived the first three heathen messengers from Herrnhuth, viz., Christian David, Matthew Stach, and Christian Stach. From this point begins the history of the Mission of the Moravian Brethren, which we may make the subject of a future sketch.

We close this account by giving Pastor Egede's own translation of the Lord's Prayer into the Greenland language.

THE LORD'S PRAYER.

NALLEKAM OKAUSIA.

Attavut killangmepotit, akkit usorolirsuk; Nallegavet aggerle; pekorset Killangme nunam etog tamaikile: Tunnisigun ullume nekiksautivnik; pissarauneta aketsorauta, pisingilaguttog aketsortivut; Ursennartomut pisitsaraunata; ajortomin annautigut: Nallegauet, Pisarlo, usornartorlo pigangaukit isukangithomun. Amen.

THE END.

S. Cowan & Co., Strathmore Printing Works, Perth.

www.ingramcontent.com/pod-product-compliance
Lightning Source LLC
Chambersburg PA
CBHW020807230426
43666CB00007B/890